beauty and the
BUSINESS

Praise for BEAUTY and the BUSINESS

"Whether starting a practice, modifying the focus of a practice, or running a mature aesthetic surgical practice, *Beauty and the Business* will make you re-evaluate your approach to the business of medicine: attracting new patients, providing service, and maintaining patient loyalty. It is a practical and outstanding text for the rapidly changing landscape of cosmetic medicine. Anyone reading it will modify some aspects of his or her approach to running an aesthetic practice."

Robert Singer, MD, FACS
Board Certified Plastic Surgeon
Singer Surgery Centre (La Jolla, CA)
Former President: American Society for Aesthetic Plastic Surgery
Former Chairman Board of Trustees: American Society of Plastic Surgeons
Former President: California Society of Plastic Surgeons
Editorial Advisory Board Chairman: *New Beauty Magazine*
Author of over 150 scientific publications in addition to major presentations at national & international Plastic Surgery meetings

"With great interest, I was given a copy of *Beauty and the Business* by Gregory Buford, M.D. and Steven House to preview. I am familiar with Dr. Buford's work in practice management and enjoy his perspective on how to succeed (he calls it "thrival") in the practice of aesthetic plastic surgery and cosmetic medicine. I find that the book contains excellent concepts of business development and management strategies that are applicable to all plastic surgeons. *Beauty and the Business* is an excellent playbook of concise chapters that cleverly address salient topics of strategy and tactics.

The business side of plastic surgery has always been of great personal interest, even more intensified when I married the banker's daughter, who shared my dream of working for myself and being able to reap the benefits of a well-run medical corporation. Like the authors of *Beauty and the Business*, we believed that the rewards of having a "best in class" performing practice create immeasurable value for patients, enhance a professional reputation, and provide sustainability in challenging economic times.

Our practice has always been in an evolutionary growth mode with regards to having a patient-centric focus, attention to business, and strategic endpoints. I think that we understood from the beginning that patients were seeking more than just episodic surgical procedures and that the nurturing of long-term relationships would reap measurable benefits. The discipline of running a successful business, humility, and avoidance of greed have been great life lessons.

Both my wife, Mary Jewell, who teaches and publishes on practice management and I believe that the concepts contained within *Beauty and the Business* should be classified as a "must read" by all plastic surgeons who want to do better. This includes young plastic surgeons that are finishing their training, devoid of business skills, heavily in debt, and with uncertain expectations of just "wanting a job".

Beauty and the Business should be read with great care, as it contains many pearls. Much of this is fairly classic material, distilled from the writing by individuals who have had landmark articles in <u>Harvard Business Review</u>: Peter Drucker, Michael Porter, Clayton Christensen, and Kim & Mauborgne of the world. There is a watershed of business strategy and insight, especially from Harvard Business Review's inexpensive offprint library.

We believe that much has changed over the last year with regards to the economic marketplace and the politics of healthcare reform. Aesthetic plastic surgery and cosmetic medicine are leading economic indicators of discretionary spending. In good times, they compete against other luxury expenditures. During recessionary times, we have found that for many patients, the inexpensive procedures that we innovated within cosmetic medicine have proven to be an area of growth. We have found that there are opportunities in the area of cost innovation, lean processes that eliminate waste and mistakes, and by offering niche procedures that differentiate our practice such as lipoabdominoplasty. By adapting to change, we have been able to meet the needs of the post-recession consumer and have a "brand" that delivers value and satisfaction in plastic surgery and cosmetic medicine.

In the post-apocalyptic era of healthcare reform, the survival of independent practices will largely depend on their ability to run a great business and have strategies to beat the tax man. *Beauty and the Business* will prove to be a great resource."

Mark L. Jewell, M.D.
Board Certified Plastic Surgeon
Private Practice (Eugene, OR)
Former President: American Society for Aesthetic Plastic Surgery 2005-2006
Assistant Clinical Professor: Department of Plastic Surgery at Oregon Health Science University
Instructor for numerous scientific courses and author of multiple scientific journal articles and book chapters including the ASPS Patient Consultation Resource Guide for Informed Consent

"Plastic Surgery offices finally have a business advisor they can count on with *Beauty and the Business* by Dr. Gregory Buford and Steven House.

Beauty and the Business is a new, state of the art book that defines the three dimensions of art, science, and business for the creation of quality service through branding and fine attention to detail. Through a series of carefully constructed chapters, the book takes the plastic surgeon and support staff by the hand and walks them down the path of defining, creating, and maintaining a "Five Star" practice based on patient and customer service. To address the fact that many old school doctors have long neglected the business of medicine, Dr. Buford has redefined the essentials of balancing the ethical practice of medicine with the management of a successful practice. How to achieve this winning combination is clearly described in *Beauty and the Business* which should be read, and re-read in order to obtain the most benefit from the multitude of useful tips provided."

Mark A. Codner, MD
Board Certified Plastic Surgeon
PACES Plastic Surgery (Atlanta, GA)
Author of over 150 national and international presentations in addition to 100 journal articles, 25 textbook chapters, and author/editor of seven books on Plastic Surgery

"*Beauty and the Business* shows us that the old adage, think before you act, has a place in aesthetic medicine. This book converts classic business models into relevant, cost-effective strategies to deliver cosmetic care that matches your audience while keeping a personal perspective. Brand recognition is emphasized throughout the book not as a gimmick but as a fundamental essential reality that has to exist in order to achieve your ultimate potential-a fact that I hold central to my practice philosophy. Regardless of your feelings about marketing, *Beauty and the Business* offers something for everyone wanting to enhance their approach to the art of aesthetic care delivery."

Julius W. Few Jr. MD
Board Certified Plastic Surgeon
The Few Institute for Aesthetic Plastic Surgery (Chicago, IL)
Developer and Director, Northwestern University Feinberg School of Medicine Aesthetic and Breast Fellowship

"Medical Training is so complex that there is too little time devoted to training new doctors on how to be "new businessman". And if running a medical practice isn't hard enough, running a totally elective consumer driven practice is twice as hard. Dr. Gregory Buford is a special individual from the "Internet generation" that has chosen a different path than the majority of plastic surgeons – a purely aesthetic surgeon with a very focused practice. His wealth of knowledge on branding, marketing, social interfacing, customer service are outstanding and have helped him build a very successful practice. His insights and personal experiences expressed through his writing will be very useful to not only the cosmetic plastic surgeon, a business man in the area of body and facial beauty, but to all doctors trying to improve their customer service, patient satisfaction, and perform cost-effective marketing."

Richard J. Greco, MD FACS
Board Certified Plastic Surgeon
The Georgia Institute for Plastic Surgery (Savannah, GA)
Member: American Society for Aesthetic Surgery
Advisory Board Member: *The Consumer Guide to Plastic Surgery*
Editor*: Emergency Plastic Surgery*
Author of over 30 scientific papers and six textbook chapters

"A pointed, thoughtful approach to the aesthetic marketplace, Dr. Gregory Buford and Steven House have given us a guide I would have dreamed of having when I started my practice. A must read for every Plastic Surgeon, both new in practice and the well established practitioner. Shape your practice, don't expect it to happen on it's own...Read on."

Michael Schwartz, MD
Board Certified Facial Plastic Surgeon
Private Practice: Westlake, CA
Facial Plastic Surgery Instructor: University of Southern California

beauty and the BUSINESS

Gregory A. Buford, MD FACS

&

Steven E. House

New York

Beauty and the Business
Practice, Profits and Productivity
Performance and Profitability

Softcover ISBN: 978-1-60037-714-3

Hardcover ISBN: 978-1-60037-715-0

Library of Congress Control Number: 2009936847

MORGAN · JAMES
THE ENTREPRENEURIAL PUBLISHER

Morgan James Publishing
1225 Franklin Ave., STE 325
Garden City, NY 11530-1693
Toll Free 800-485-4943
www.MorganJamesPublishing.com

In an effort to support local communities, raise awareness and funds, Morgan James Publishing donates one percent of all book sales for the life of each book to Habitat for Humanity. Get involved today, visit **www.HelpHabitatForHumanity.org**.

"Toto, I've a feeling that we're not in Kansas anymore"

Dorothy (The Wizard of Oz)

FOREWORD

I opened a prepublication draft of *BEAUTY and the BUSINESS* with great anticipation. Having heard Greg Buford speak on practice branding and positioning several times, I was very impressed with his incisive comments, and looked forward to a more complete exposition of his views. I was not disappointed and roared through the book he authored with Steven House over two evenings. With Buford's firsthand experience shaping his own practice, and House's savvy analysis and business skills, they make a great team.

While the emphasis of the book is transforming a focused aesthetic practice from an aspiration into a thriving business enterprise, the larger goal is to create personal happiness and fulfillment: for both patient/client and practitioner. With the current luxury goods down market mentality of "survival", their concept of "thrival" is refreshing and inspiring—being able to select what you do, and which clients you will serve, and making a well compensated and fulfilling success out of it. Clearly practitioner success and happiness (or their antithesis) is genetically linked to that of the client, and the analysis of enhancing and solidifying this connection is the essence of the book.

Just as this book is an excellent collaboration, successful practice is a team effort. The physician "coach" has to become clear on the strengths of the practice to ensure that there are skilled players on the bench. The physician manager must take a much broader approach to defining the "game plan" for the practice, and be even more aware of the strengths and weaknesses of the competition than in the past. As Buford points out, most plastic surgeons focus only on the medical aspects of their practice that occupied so much of their training. But this is like a team that can only play defense. To really be in the "game" the modern physician must have a well conceived and executed offense, in the form of a branding and positioning plan, in order to achieve its goals.

As a practicing plastic surgeon over the last thirty years, I have certainly watched a seismic shift in how practices conceive and manage their public face. Given the large number of truly ineffective or offensive marketing efforts I have seen—many of them displayed not only on individual but also on collective, corporate sponsored web sites—there is a very large potential market for the tight analysis and practical suggestions in *BEAUTY and the BUSINESS*. Business success is much more than smiling models, pastel colors, and over-bloated claims and testimonials. It takes real work, not chaotic energy chasing a vague shifting shadow of the consumer.

Buford and House provide the methods and tools in short well written chapters, with almost web-page like impact, that are concise but filled with personal experience and practical examples. They elucidate lessons not only from the cosmetic surgery space, but also by incorporating experience relative to parallel industries and products. The rich references are up to date, using real practice data from Plastic Surgery organizations and other current publications. The graphic aids are solid and weave the compelling story of success from the analysis of practice and target client base, the conception of practice philosophy and branding, to the execution of a marketing and patient happiness and retention program.

I found the tone of the book to be philosophical and high minded which was much more interesting and compelling than a technical "how to" marketing manual. The advice is as sound for a mature surgeon reassessing their mid career practice strategy as it is mandatory for a young surgeon just entering practice and overwhelmed with trying to master the practice and the business simultaneously. In fact, *BEAUTY and the BUSINESS* would make a great addition to the curriculum of most training programs.

Happiness and success in any endeavor is never a matter of chance, but the result of careful analysis in addition to planning and execution of a winning strategy. This book helps a surgeon determine just what makes them happiest, and which clients they have the best chance of satisfying. In *BEAUTY and the BUSINESS*, the notion of "thrival" (happy patients and fulfilled practitioners) is a great goal. And with this book in hand, its achievement is within view.

Bruce L. Cunningham, MD
President, American Society of Plastic Surgeons (ASPS) – 2006
Chair, American Board of Plastic Surgery - 2004

PREFACE

"Better to pass boldly into that other world, in the full glory of some passion, than fade and wither dismally with age."

James Joyce

Since the beginning, the healthcare industry has practiced a self-imposed moratorium on doing business and physicians have been encouraged to not address the business side of the delivery of their Oath. And yet if today's physicians aren't attentive to the business aspect of their practice, it's a sure thing they won't be practicing for long. And then who loses?

The concept for this book began several years ago during my residency training. In no uncertain terms, I was specifically instructed to not think of medicine as a business. As a surgical resident, I was surrounded by mentors whose appointment was to teach surgical technique. And while they stressed the importance of proper credentialing, the subject of money was avoided at all cost, not unlike the uncomfortable feeling in a restaurant when the waitress announces that the lobster served that evening is "market price." If you had to ask, then maybe you were in the wrong restaurant; so you just didn't ask. You just sweated the amount (particularly on an intern's pay) until the check was presented. The message implied to us was that someone else would manage the money—a practice manager, for example. And so when patients asked what a treatment would cost, we were instructed to defer that detail to someone in accounting.

So after years of hard work, long hours and endless studying, I was unceremoniously dropped into private practice where I found out that even though I had to assume risk for the business, my staff all had to be paid first leaving me to be the last one to get any money. The fact remained that there were no guarantees I'd even paid for my services, or anything, for that matter. To even open the doors of a practice you have to commit to paying full-time reception help, nursing, and space costs before you know when your first paying patient will arrive. Even then, there are no guarantees that payment due from those first patients will be on time for you to pay your staff, your office space lease, and or your basic living expenses.

Like many young associates, I began by casting a wide net seeking to fill my appointment book. I didn't turn away patients whether treating them would be a profitable use of my time or not. In observing my peers, it did not take very long for me to recognize that some aimed to make the most of their training and career; others were just filling time in between graduation and retirement. Those who were enthusiastic and excited about the work they were able to do were rewarded well financially for it. Sadly, the majority of physicians embraced the "Field of Dreams" mentality— hanging a shingle and waiting and hoping clients would come. As you can imagine, results were highly inconsistent and in most cases very poor. The defining characteristic of the successful practice seemed to be a combination of strategic planning, marketing execution and recognition that no doctor has an infinite earning capacity because no matter what we do, there are only 24 hours in a day.

Doctors who make the most of their time choose first to do things for clients that make the best medical sense. But they also consider what make the best financial sense for both the patient and themselves. In training, we were always taught to do what is right for the client and never taught to concern ourselves with profitability. But one of the most difficult early steps in your practice is knowing when to say no and when to say yes based on the profitability of your answer. This insight is cultivated as you gain experience and unfortunately can cause many early missteps that may result in the loss of both time and revenue.

I did not start my practice with a business manual like this in hand. I suffered along with the rest of my peers until I learned that the successful practitioner did not cast fate to the wind but instead proactively charted a carefully designed course engineered for success. Operating without a strategic endpoint in mind is like trying to drive somewhere without actually knowing where you want to go having never been there and expecting to arrive on time, without frustration. Typical business environments would have you assigned to a mentor but in the world of cosmetic medicine all the mentors who could potentially help you are probably your competition.

Over the last decade, I have consumed every marketing and practice building resource available. I spent nights in the library researching business strategies and essentially creating my own mission statement. I learned everything I could about how to build a business that would survive any market condition and then how to sustain and grow that business. I also learned how to manage my time so that I can add capacity to my business, and fill that capacity the way I want to keep client satisfaction and my financial results both in mind. Most of my colleagues laughed at my new ideas until, years later, when my practice had grown from a fledging entry level endeavor into a highly successful cash-only elective enterprise. In eight short years, I've built a career that now allows me to do exactly what I want: not accept insurance and actually enjoy what I do. I have patients who are thrilled with what they get when they come to my practice. On a daily basis, I literally change people's lives by the work I do. For some, the results restore lost confidence while for others it simply grants them confidence they never had. In many cases they come into my office with their heads down not wanting to be seen. But when they leave, they smile, hold their head high, and proceed to talk to everyone with a new dose of confidence.

We all have the choice between thriving and surviving. I choose to thrive. If that is your goal, it will require a paradigm shift to reach a state of what I call "thrival". Simply stated, a state of thrival is a position where your practice is not only surviving, it is thriving. I don't want to peak once and fall back or have peaks and valleys. The best case scenario for me is a practice that never stops growing in the areas of client satisfaction and profitability. But to achieve this will require you as a practitioner to adopt new methodologies and embrace an entirely new way of thinking.

Unfortunately, the problem begins early. Most medical students don't instinctively understand how to run a business. Add to this the fact medical schools and residencies focus predominantly on the clinical side of medicine—how to make a diagnosis and how to cure disease. In reality, the physician as businessman has always existed; he just hasn't been effective. The spirit of this book was born out of a desire to eliminate the frustration that comes from working within a broken system and hopefully to propose ways in which to more effectively structure, grow, and build a successful business.

If you are simply looking for a busy practice, this book is not for you. If you want to create a top performing aesthetic practice clinically and financially, read on. If you dare to enter the highly competitive marketplace, capture market share in the specific areas of practice you prefer, and celebrate the financial rewards that come with education, labor and applied new thinking, then this is your book. At times this book may seem rudimentary, but these basic principles are intended to support your core competency while reducing your risk of failure and enhancing your chances of success. If you use this book as a roadmap to enable you to develop goals, strategy and execution, you're bound to reap the same or even better benefits then I have. Remember that while your goals are critical my hope is that you will experience joy and pride in the journey.

After a decade of learning on the job with successes and failures I have come to the point where I feel a unified sense of who I am and where I am going. Satisfaction has been achieved in great part by choosing to do what I like to do and eliminating what I do not. In the early years of my practice, while I enjoyed the reconstructive insurance-based medical component, I was continually frustrated by the many hoops I had to jump through to get reimbursed for the work I did and the long hours wasted arguing with insurance companies. This same frustration is being felt on a national level as the medical system progressively becomes more challenging from the standpoint of inadequate reimbursement and increasing medico-legal exposure. As a result, the best and the brightest are no longer targeting medicine as a profession but instead rallying towards other fields. The pay-off is seemingly no longer there. I would disagree. I have truly enjoyed what I do and am continuously grateful for the lives that I have touched and the clients with whom I have worked. No other profession allows us to see so deeply into the human spirit and affect such a dramatic change. For this, I am eternally grateful. My goal is that this book will help you rekindle the flame and see medicine in an entirely different light. Now let's begin your journey to build a more rewarding practice and the life you dreamed about when you made that important choice to serve patients as a doctor.

—Greg

My 25 years in healthcare have included time with major imaging vendors such as Philips Medical Systems and GE Healthcare. During this, I spent ten years working in healthcare IT including physician office billing systems, electronic medical records in offices and hospitals, computerized physician order entry systems, patient safety initiatives, and interoperability. I have also spent the past three years engaged in web and referral-based marketing inside physician practices. From those experiences, I learned that there is a right time and a right way to market your business and that often varies depending on many factors. Building a business from a set of unique skills is really not that difficult. But marketing that business and making it profitable are another thing entirely. Marketing is an art when you have an entire team of highly educated marketing people to do it. When it is only you it is like trying to make a stick figure look like a masterpiece.

I joined with Dr. Buford in writing this book because I believe that all specialties, cosmetic plastic surgery included, need to understand how to improve the business side of their practice and demonstrate the value they bring to their consumers. We live in an important time in history where it is critical to market your practice to self-paying patients regardless of whether or not you also take insurance. Reimbursements are being cut yearly and will continue to do so based on the rising cost of healthcare, an aging population and the explosive growth of the obesity epidemic and its associated costs. So to live your own personal dream as a physician, you can either find ways to expand your profitable revenue or choose to down-size your dream.

It has taken me 25 years in the business of healthcare to fully realize that healthcare is not usually run as a business. At least it is certainly not run that way in most cases. To begin with, the notion of healthcare as a business is not taught in many medical schools. You can get an MHA, which appears to be an MBA for healthcare, but keep in mind that those initials stand for

Masters in Health Administration not Masters in Healthcare Business. On the other hand, I do know many very well qualified hospital administrators who are sound business people so I don't want you to think that I am completely negative on the subject. But the time has come to emphasize healthcare as a business for a number of good reasons.

According to some estimates, healthcare now represents nearly 14% of the gross US domestic product (GDP). As part of that cost it adds more then $2000 to the price of a car. This doesn't even take into account the coming genetic revolution that will, by some estimates, drive healthcare costs to account for up to 50% of the GDP by mid-century. Add to this an increasing obese population and their attendant costs and the healthcare situation becomes more and more strained. The United States and World Economies alike cannot sustain an environment where the cost of healthcare continues to climb at 14% per year for very long because it takes funding away from other important objectives such as alternative energy. The net result will be continuous cuts in the cost of healthcare and physician practices are a big part of that cost.

We are writing this book to help you overcome this environment using two primary objectives. Both objectives are based on the simple equation that:

Profitability = Revenue – Cost

To maintain profitability (your net income) in the face of declining reimbursements, you must either increase revenue or cut costs or both. If you have been in practice for awhile you have probably cut your costs as far as you can already so that leaves you with a strategy that must grow revenue. The two objectives we pursue are therefore to grow profitable revenue while increasing practice capacity so that your costs can remain static. In this book we will emphasize the importance of identifying find profitable service lines for your patients and will discuss the need for you realize that your profitability is in part based upon your ability to service these patients even if it doesn't seem like you have the time to do so.

A major issue facing healthcare in the United States is some of our potential clients are choosing competitors outside our country. Outsourcing of healthcare to countries such as India and Brazil is becoming more common every day. And the reason? Cost. Cost is the measuring stick in healthcare whether you are deciding on an insurance plan or provider or if you are pursuing elective surgery. Cost has become the basis in today's economy because physicians are not taught how to demonstrate value in what they do and they are certainly never instructed on how to elevate the argument above just cost.

Capitalism is based on value and in healthcare we have ignored it due to a lack of training in the business of healthcare. With that, we are also seeing a movement toward consumerism in healthcare which will mean that clients will have more of their own money at stake in whom they choose to get their healthcare from. These consumers are used to buying based upon perceived value and if your practice isn't strongly promoting its' value, then you will ultimately lose market share.

My hope is that this book will confirm what you already know and compel you to more profitably grow your business. It is also my hope that you will take the lessons that Dr. Buford and I have learned apart and together to expand in new areas of value creation and strategy and accomplish the objective of profitably growing your healthcare business.

The one thing we do know is that action leads to results. Absence of action leads you nowhere and in most cases actually sets you back. Do not read this book if you are not planning to take action because it is written with actionable data. If you are not sure about how to proceed, contact us. Our information is provided at the back of this book and we would love to speak with you. Touch base with either one of us and our team will be happy to help you move forward. I believe in true value and I do not want anyone to read this book without getting value from its contents. Action, based upon relevant knowledge, is the best game plan in every case and that is why you should read on. Now let's get started......

—**Steve**

ACKNOWLEDGEMENTS

As a child, I spent a great deal of time in libraries reading, exploring, and gaining knowledge about the world. And during this time, my teachers were my inspiration and the driving force behind the passion that I had and always will have for the written word. I learned early on that the human experience is universal and that definition of self is an on-going but exciting process during which passion and hunger for self-awareness serve as integral catalysts along this great adventure. As a literature major at the University of California, San Diego my intellectual curiosity literally exploded as I dove headfirst into the Humanities and learned from both the antiquities and the contemporary movements and ultimately began to shape myself as a person.

Although it would be impossible to name every artist who impacted me, I specifically owe a great debt of gratitude to F. Scott Fitzgerald, Jorge Luis Borges, and Gabriel Garcia Marquez. Their works drove me to question the position of the individual being within the world and taught me that with faith, passion, and purpose, I could accomplish anything I set my mind to. And it was during these years that I begin an assimilation of both science and art into the drive towards self awareness.

As a result of recent changes in my life, this passion has been reawakened. And as a result, I have never been more fulfilled as a person and a human being while realizing that there is significantly more greatness to come. And the greatest outcome from these changes has been the inspiration for me to move forward with the writing of this book.

But none of this would have been possible without the steadfast and loving support of my parents, Gary and Betty. I can never thank them enough for everything they did to help get me to this point. This book and the blood, sweat, and tears it took to get me this far is dedicated to them. I would also like to acknowledge my physician mentors and my wonderful staff who have put up with me over these years. You all have been a great source of inspiration and support and I am a better person for having met you all.

—Gregory A. Buford, MD FACS

The teachings of Jack Canfield, Andy Andrews, and Tony Robbins have played a significant role in my personal development process. I have read their books and want to especially acknowledge Success Principles by Jack, The Traveler's Gift by Andy, and Unlimited Power by Tony. Their teachings and coaching, along with the encouragement of my father have lead me to seek wisdom through reading and experience and those experiences have allowed me to gain insight in to how to run a business, use marketing to be successful, and driven me to compete at the highest level of everything I do. This book represents a combination of my own thoughts and ideas, along with the inspiration of Jack, Andy, and Tony, that have been tried and successfully produced results. My commitment to being the best in all that I do come from my father who is my hero and I dedicate this to him.

—Steven E. House, BSBA

TABLE OF CONTENTS

SECTION 1

DEFINING GREATNESS

CHAPTER 1

WHAT DOES GREATNESS LOOK LIKE?

"Be not afraid of greatness; some are born great, some achieve greatness, and others have greatness thrust upon them."

William Shakespeare

In setting out to write this book, my goal was to explore the new Cosmetic Marketplace, the new Cosmetic Patient, and to better define strategies for achieving success given an entirely new paradigm. In so doing, I wanted to incorporate practice innovations that had worked successfully for me while spending equal time on those that did not. And I also wanted to include a sampling of successful Plastic Surgery practices from various socioeconomic zones across the country and identify pearls and tips they found helpful.

My goal was not to offer a single approach but, instead, an amalgam of different approaches and tactics used successfully across different practices. Because although I have enjoyed success, my way is certainly not the only way and I wanted to see what strategies others had found useful. And that is where I hit a wall.

I hand-selected a dozen thriving Plastic Surgery practices across the country and asked them for their thoughts. And almost without exception, my responses were either left unanswered or I was given some reason why they would not be a good "role model". In other cases, I was told that they were simply too busy. And that is when the light bulb went on.

For most people in the aesthetic marketplace, competition is difficult if not downright stifling. And most will try anything to achieve some modicum of success. And once that strategy has been formed, we are not willing to let the proverbial "cat out of the bag" as to what actually led to our success. And that is understandable. One practitioner in a large metropolitan area actually recounted his concerns with sharing his tips. He had had enough of his competition copying his ads, stealing his promotions, and even going so far as to videotape his own office. He at least had the courage to explain why he didn't wish to participate instead of just saying no.

I can understand the hesitancy to relinquish your secrets…to effectively open the door to the vault of the truths of what has worked for you and what has not worked. And I can understand the initial impulse to avoid sharing that with what may effectively be your competition. But that is where I politely disagree.

Aesthetic procedures are taught on a daily basis around the world and will continue to be shared. And residency programs will continue to offer the bare nuts and bolts of practicing medicine but they have never discussed the true practice of medicine…and that is bad business. A well thought out approach to Branding, Marketing, and Advertising your practice will strategically highlight your strengths and your differences from the rest of the competition. And at its core, its emphasis will be you. And that can never be stolen or reproduced. If your branding is strong, it should stand the test of time and the onslaught of your competition. If not, it will not. And so while I may offer a few templates here and there, the true focus of this book is not to create carbon copy practices—no matter how successful---but instead to help position you to create your own look, your own feel, and to guide you down a path that will eventually lead to financial and personal success.

And so from this first rejection, what I lost in participation of my peers, I gained in clarity and focus of mission….both of which over the ensuing chapters I hope to pass along to you.

CHAPTER SUMMARY POINTS:

- Never be afraid to teach others. You are where you are today because of the wisdom of your mentors. Pass this knowledge along and the rewards you will reap will be endless.

- Branding, marketing, and advertising are the lost keys to practice growth we were never given during training. Credibly executed, they are the foundation for success.

Chapter 2

PATHS TO GREATNESS BEGIN WITH A STRONG FOUNDATION

*"Great things are not done by impulse, but by a
series of small things brought together."*

Vincent Van Gogh

For many years, the American medical profession was a source of respect, growth, and reverence. Physicians were respected for their work ethic, their dedication, and their ability for delayed gratification. Unfortunately, these same traits are now proving to be their undoing. The new American physician has changed. Once populated by highly motivated overachievers, residency programs are now seeing a dramatic change in their applicants. Applicants are seeking careers with more control over work hours and working conditions and are no longer willing to accept an all-encompassing career that dictates their every move. This growing movement within the medical profession is becoming stronger with the end result that applicants are seeking a more proactive role in the creation of their identity, workplace condition and overall lifestyle. The new American physician was borne out of years of delayed gratification and from the ashes of crippled marriages and absentee existence. Trainees entering the marketplace see their peers in other industries not only entering careers earlier but also making substantially more money in the long run often with considerably more control of their career path and their lives in general. An offshoot of this movement was the creation of the aesthetic marketplace. This elective-based procedural marketplace was cultivated and grown from decades of frustration within the medical industry as a whole in response to both a need previously unmet as well as a lifestyle previously unattainable.

Most current political debates begin with a scathing assessment of the breakdown of the American healthcare system. To politicians, the system is broken and must be fixed. The common theme suggested is of a system that is costing more and more money and budgets which need to be slashed and trimmed. Unfortunately, the popular target for reform has consistently been physician reimbursement. At the same time that reimbursement continues to get cut to manage budget shortfalls, physician's cost of living has not correspondingly gone down. And so physician salaries continue to decline as long as this short-sighted mentality remains popular. Add to this a climate of increasing medico-legal exposure and a professional environment less supportive of the individual physician, and the end result is increased stress and progressively decreasing job satisfaction.

With the emergence of this elective marketplace comes a new set of rules governing creation, maintenance, and growth of a medical practice. It is no longer acceptable to merely hang your shingle and wait for clients to come. As a practitioner in this new environment, you must rise to challenges which have always existed, but which in recent years have become far more complicated as less pay has become the standard for the same amount of work. We will continue to lose our flexibility to offer loss leading procedures and technologies that may in fact really help our patients. Without reasonable reimbursement, we simply cannot take the risk. The solution is to aggressively market your business and identify profitable service lines. Twenty years ago, it was considered taboo to market your skills; now for most practices, it is the cost of doing business. If we are going to head in this direction and utilize these new practice building tools, we need to understand what they can and cannot do to most effectively harness their creative powers and effectively compete in this aesthetic marketplace.

The first step in building your business is the clear and simple recognition that your practice is a business. The first question you should ask is, "What specific structure should I use for my business?" Whether or not you decide to join a partnership or go it on your own is really a question of your individual practice style and your financial situation starting out. There are advantages and disadvantages to both sides but in the end it really depends upon the practice atmosphere that you seek and ultimately how much control you wish to exercise over its direction. Solo practice can be enthralling and will ultimately give you complete control (both good and bad) over the direction of your practice along with total financial responsibility. It can also be isolated and lonely as you move from the camaraderie of residency training to the world of solo practice. I have personally enjoyed working in a group setting since it has given me the ability to bounce ideas off of my partners and consult with them on challenging cases. But it has also been difficult when my marketing ideas have clashed with theirs. To address these differences, I developed a practice within a practice where my individual entity effectively exists as a free-standing business under the umbrella of a master group entity. This has allowed me the opportunity to create a look and feel representative of my goals and designs and to chart a course entirely designed around these goals while still enjoying the benefits of participating with the framework of a group.

Once you have chosen your practice structure, you must begin developing your client base. You may notice that I use the term "client" and not "patient". This seemingly basic choice of a word is actually a powerfully reflective change in the mindset of the aesthetic practitioner. The simple decision to address customers as clients reflects a shift away from traditional practice dynamics. And this critical difference solidifies a mindset within your practice where experience is recognized as an attribute equal to results. To better understand this, we can thank the folks at Starbucks.

Years ago, for many Americans, coffee was considered to be a simple delivery instrument for caffeine. That idea was inexorably altered with the explosive growth of Starbucks. This Seattle-based company took a common drink and built an entire culture of experience around it. Clients do not simply purchase coffee from Starbucks; they buy into the distinctive look of the surroundings, the cheeriness of the barista behind the counter, and the variety of the menu...in essence, the experience. In much the same way, successful medical practices are quickly realizing that they have a lot to learn from the Starbuck's experience. If you think that aesthetic clients are looking only for the best results, you are sadly mistaken. While clients seek certain outcomes, they are also seeking an experience. Clients know coming into your practice means they are going to spend a significant amount of money but they are willing to do so for the positive changes you will help them achieve as well as the environment they will find within your office. It is different than going to a traditional medical office setting to be treated for to an upper respiratory infection because in our case the client is paying the entire bill with no assistance from insurance. In many cases they will pay you more as a practitioner than they will pay for everything else they buy with the exception of their home and their car. Rewarding them with a sterile medical experience will certainly not win you the business you seek. Top practices have a nurse welcome each patient as soon as they enter the waiting room to let that person know they are glad to see them. At the same time, the nurse asks them if they need a bottle of water, reading material, or anything else that will make them comfortable. They will also ask how the client is and if they are on a particular time crunch. Although this may sound trivial, accepting that clients are drawn to experiential medical treatment as much as they are to the experience of a cup of java in the morning is the first step in identifying and optimally addressing your client base.

The topic of strategic marketing can easily be confused with the idea that big nets catch more fish. We will help you understand that more fish does not necessarily translate to desired fish. In this case, marketing doesn't end at the moment when a potential client first enters your office and becomes a paying client. This is the point where the most important marketing begins. We will spend time in later chapters showing you the value of one-on-one marketing that can expand the number of services lines that a client is able to access within your practice as well as the depth they go into each line. The right marketing directed at the right client improves return on investment but allows you to build your practice in a carefully focused and coordinated direction.

So now that we recognize the potential for focused experiential marketing, what strategies should be undertaken to actually attain clients? The basis for client acquisition begins with focused branding, marketing and advertising. Once you've established the brand you want to be—the look and feel of your marketing pieces that tell the world of potential clients who you are and what you do best—it's time to embrace the two most effective sources of client acquisition: website presence and word-of-mouth referrals. The most expensive lessons that I learned in building my practice were which strategies proved to be most effective in achieving acceptable return on investment. Very early on, I did what everyone else does and I bought into the idea that I needed to purchase a large Yellow Pages advertisement. I quickly learned that the type of client I was looking for did not use a three-pound book with tiny type as a resource. Instead, my Yellow Pages presence was attracting the proverbial "shopper". While these difficult-to-please clients may contribute to practice growth early on, they can also be extremely frustrating to work with. You goal should be to create a practice that allows you to pick the type of client you want to work with versus taking any client that walks through the door in order to keep busy. Don't forget that your goal is a continuously growing profitable business with the highest level of client satisfaction. Shoppers are interested in getting the best deal possible and are not afraid to use hardball negotiation tactics in the quest to save a few dollars by eating into or eliminating your profit. They also tend to be among your least satisfied clients in the long run, as well as the most demanding. In short, I recommend avoiding this particular client type as they are only a short term solution. Overall, they are wholly ineffective for true practice building as they'll usually migrate to the next practice for the latest discounted deal and they virtually never become a quality referral source.

Once you've identified the type of client you are marketing to, what medium can you actually use to reach them? It depends on your market. In most cases today, the internet has become a first stop for shoppers looking for any type of service. This fact alone creates the need for every aesthetic practice to build and maintain a good website. An effective website serves multiple functions. It is the cornerstone of experiential marketing and educates your potential client on the look, feel, and personality of your practice. As such, every detail in the design of your website is critical in conveying your true practice philosophy. The basic colors of your site suggest a specific personality and educate your consumer to the experience that they can expect from your individual practice. The same applies to the choice of language used as website copy. In appealing to a select client persona, specific copy must be targeted to a specific audience. To accomplish this, you need to identify the age, gender, race, education and socioeconomic makeup of your target client. While I don't advocate speaking down to your clients, direct language to their specific needs. If your target consumer is a 25-35 year-old female with a high school education, speak to them in a way they can understand. The same applies if you are targeting a more mature, educated audience. This philosophy also applies to the overall look and feel of your site. In general terms, know your audience and develop your site accordingly.

One simple strategy that you must do is to review competitive websites that rank at or near the top of search engines. There is a reason they are there and you need to know that reason. Keep in mind that the primary purpose for the website is to drive targeted traffic to your practice but if done right your website will also cause some potential customers to consider a service they didn't go to your website to specifically find. An example of this would be if they were concerned about fine lines and wrinkles and were looking for a botulinum toxin type A product but while on your site realized that they may also want to use a filler to replace lost facial volume. Your website should lead them to the conclusion that you care about their particular problem or need and that you are very good at addressing it.

Another important source of new patients should be your existing client base. Who better to promote your services than someone who has already seen what you can do. Keep strict records of referral sources and be quick to reward them. For every new client in my office, we identify their source of referral and routinely track who refers what and how often. We've found that rewarding referring clients with beautiful floral arrangements works very well. Who doesn't appreciate an unexpected delivery of flowers? Before each new patient leaves my office, we make sure the referring source is identified, recorded, and a floral arrangement sent to them the following morning. This seemingly basic approach has proven quite effective among our clients and has received overwhelmingly positive feedback. If you consider that $50 to $75 spent on something so basic may cultivate the production of additional clients (who often spend anywhere from hundreds to thousands of dollars), the return on investment for this simple gesture is tremendously positive. This basic approach has been so effective that I have actually eliminated most print advertising in favor of spending marketing dollars on directly rewarding referring clients. I have found that this is beneficial not only from a standpoint of ROI but, more importantly, it has allowed me to cultivate a very positive relationship with clients on a much deeper level than any print advertisement could ever achieve.

Database marketing is another highly effective source of marketing and can be taken to new levels when you consider the latest email marketing technologies available. I personally do not like receiving standard mail and will throw away bulk mailings before giving them a single glance. In talking to other people, their reactions are often very similar. As such, I have eliminated any mailings in lieu of online communication. Regular updates are sent to my client-base via email informing them of current incentives, upcoming events, or simply as a way to remind them of the services that I offer. Advantages to this marketing approach greatly outweigh those of conventional bulk mailings. Just as with bulk mail however, you must manage the number of times you contact a client with promotional offers and information so that you don't upset them and cause them to ignore you all together. Getting direct feedback from your clients on the emails you do send them is a good way to track this. And using an individualized call to action for each specific marketing campaign allows you to identify truly how effective each effort really is.

The only cost to using email marketing is a small subscription fee to a bulk emailer (often less than $200/year). By sending information to a client in email format, you are providing a medium that is much easier to pass on to their friends and family than a conventional mailing. And encouraging them to forward incentives on to their friends (and of course rewarding them for doing so), you are effectively creating and promoting a viral marketing campaign.

The exciting thing about electronic marketing is that for many of these strategies you are only limited by your own creativity. One way to grow your client base is to identify strategic partners and create joint marketing campaigns that provide higher combined value to your clients then with either partner implementing a stand-alone campaign. The same person interested in addressing facial aging may also be interested in teeth whitening or Lasik surgery as a way to provide them with a more comprehensive and more natural look. By working with strategic partners, you are opening up your database to additional incentives while at the same time expanding your own database by cross-promoting to an entirely different list of clientele. The end result is expanded reach for minimal capital expenditure.

Now that you've decided to enter the world of elective medicine, what are the barriers to entry? Competition is always a barrier and in this case you will see that a good percentage of your colleagues, previously involved in insurance-based medicine, have now become your direct competition. But while competition for discretionary spending will continue to increase, the aging population is driving the demand for aesthetic services to an even broader audience. This increases your overall client base with available money to spend on your services. So while the pie may be sliced into more pieces, the calories per piece will ultimately be richer.

As the field of aesthetic medicine has grown, it has drawn more and more attention away from the "core" fields of Plastic Surgery, Facial Plastic Surgery and Aesthetic Dermatology and attracted competition from OB-Gyn's, Family Practitioner's and even Emergency Room Physicians who have introduced aesthetic options to their service menus. And this introduction of aesthetic services into non-typical medical office environments is not going to slow down. On the contrary, it will pick up momentum as time goes on. In the next twenty years, due to increasing pressure from the insurance companies, declining reimbursement, movement toward consumerism in healthcare and increasing medico legal exposure, growth in competition will be the norm. Inherent in this growth is the expansion of groups such as the American Academy of Cosmetic Medicine (AACM) , American Academy of Aesthetic Medicine (AAAM), and American Society of Laser Medicine and Surgery (ASLMS) both in number of members and in political power, much to the chagrin of first-to-market institutions such as American Society of Plastic Surgeons (ASPS) and American Society for Aesthetic Plastic Surgery (ASAPS). There is gold in this market and all of these groups want a piece of it.

A profitably growing practice is not the competition, but, more importantly, value based outcomes and patient safety. Every market has a buyer and seller. In deciding how to create real value that out performs competition, you must understand the client's perspective on value. Of course they want you to do great work and make them look and feel fantastic, but there is more to it than that. As we stated earlier, it is about the entire experience from the first contact to your website to the day they show up for a consult to the depth of the relationship you and your staff develop with them that will get you the amount of business you want. Don't ever lose sight of the fact that the client determines the value of the outcome…not you.

On the patient safety side, you as a physician provider of services impart a great deal of impact. But whether or not, as a Plastic Surgeon, I accept that a non-core physician, in terms of Aesthetic Medicine (or physician extender), may be performing elective aesthetic procedures, the bottom line is that the current medical atmosphere and growing competition has and will continue to create a supply of practitioners who will perform these types of procedures and patient safety will be at potentially greater risk. Competing on the issue of patient safety, given an environment of varying degrees of competency and training, will force the industry to create standards that deal with the realization that complications within the elective arena overall will occur with both non-core and core-trained aesthetic practitioners. And so the need for effective, comprehensive, and standardized training in elective procedures is now not a question of if, but when. It is vital to patients and to the growth of the entire industry that those who are entering this arena must be trained in the safe and effective performance of these procedures. Major complications and patient safety incidents will hurt not only those who perform poorly but can potentially affect the image of the entire industry in all potential patients' eyes. When tainted Tylenol killed 3 people in the 80's, the entire over the counter industry suffered jointly because people perceived those products to be unsafe. The same type of reaction will happen if there were too many negative incidents in the aesthetic industry caused by untrained or poorly trained individuals.

Anyone entering the aesthetic elective arena must also be realistic as to what procedure and services they should and should not be performing. While suggestions of a turf war abound, there are certainly arguments to be made for training, experience, and the transparency of published outcomes as a means to insure patient safety. And so for both the aesthetically as well as the non-aesthetically trained practitioner, adequate exposure to current methods is requisite for minimizing complications and maintaining patient safety associated with cosmetic procedures and assuring positive patient outcomes.

Another hot topic involves the increasing need for medical supervision of physician extenders as well as stopgaps for avoiding or at least minimizing medical complications. To this end, transparency on medical training, background, and experience, is now being evaluated.

The state of Florida recently enacted legislation requiring those practitioners who advertise Board Certification to identify in what particular field they are actually board certified. Although this may be taken as a swipe against the non-core physician, in reality it is a very important step forward in protecting the patient. Transparency is simply a means with which to advertise training credentials and experience and better educate our client base. As a Plastic Surgeon, I have to accept that there may be non-core physicians achieving equal or better results than myself. If that is the case, then the issue of continued training falls squarely on my shoulders as well as the responsibility for me to sharpen my skills through hands-on mentored training. In addition, as the field of Aesthetic Medicine continues to expand, the importance of open lines of communication and dissemination of training techniques and standardization will continue to increase. The end result will be a more effective and, most importantly, a safer operative environment for the aesthetic client.

CHAPTER SUMMARY POINTS:

- You run a business. You also treat patients. But keep in mind, you run a business.

- Hanging a shingle only gives you a shingle. You must deliberately seek out patients specific to your type of aesthetic practice to effectively build your practice.

- When executed in a credible and ethical manner, strategic marketing is a powerful tool for spreading the word about you and your practice.

- Patients are looking not only for results, they are seeking an experience. Provide it and they will come.

- Your existing clients are an important resource for the cultivation of new clients.

- Be transparent. Your training background and results are important in differentiating your from the competition. Let your clients know this.

Chapter 3

CURRENT TRENDS

"In any moment of decision the best thing you can do is the right thing, the next best thing is the wrong thing, and the worst thing you can do is nothing."

Theodore Roosevelt

Baby Boomers are reaching the age where the battle to look good has become an all out war… a war they won't except defeat in easily because they simply want to look good. In fact, they want to be active and look good all the way to their graves. The increased popularity of cosmetic procedures stems from a number of several factors but the pure and simple fact is that looking good is no longer a relative term. Telling someone that "she looks good for her age" is likely to get you a slap instead of a thank you. She looks good without qualification to her age is now the only acceptable answer. In examining why consumer trends have shifted, we must look to both ends of the age spectrum. On one end, the population is living longer and living better. The prospect of wearing heavy makeup and only going out when lighting levels are in your best interest is being traded in for BOTOX Cosmetic, the newest filler, and a nip and tuck here and there. Wanting to be seen at any hour of the day instead of being forced into a sedentary lifestyle has become the norm. And with this more active lifestyle comes the need to not only do more but also look good while you're doing it.

On the other end of the spectrum are the younger clients who have realized much earlier than we, that prophylactic measures to address the aging process are essential in helping stave off more aggressive procedures down the road--an ounce of prevention if you will. With all due respect to George Hamilton and Coco Chanel, dark tans and the wrinkles they helped create are no longer sexy. Since incorporating injectables into my practice, I have seen a distinctive trend on either side of this age spectrum for adoption of facial injectables in combination with medical skincare and laser rejuvenation. For those who still want the tan they also expect that a couple of times a year they can get a laser treatment and have the age spots removed so they can do it all over again.

Another explanation for this increasing adoption is not only more effective consumer education among all age ranges but also more financial availability and the growing acceptance that it is okay to spend money to look better. Add to this the fact that the American pocketbook is now being assisted by readily available financing and the aesthetic marketplace is now open to a whole new audience. And even as the economy tightens, mortgages foreclose, and consumer confidence wanes, financing continues for this aesthetic consumer and with it growth of the aesthetic marketplace. The new face of cosmetic surgery now encompasses a much wider audience with respect to age, gender, ethnicity, and socioeconomic means than ever before. Whether we like it or not, we compete everyday for the right jobs, the right deals, and the right social connections. Looking young and fresh at every age gives us an advantage in life's natural competition.

As the divorce rate continues to affect more than half of our population, and men and women re-enter single life, we find ourselves competing in an arena which favors the youthful, relaxed appearance. As such, more and more people are increasingly turning to less invasive means to turn back the clock. On the other hand those individuals lucky enough to survive as a couple, are finding themselves looking to the aesthetic industry with the aim of not only growing old together but also looking good doing it.

So in this growing marketplace what are people actually looking for? One of the more popular trends is a rapidly increasing emphasis on non-surgical procedures. According to ASAPS, the top non-invasive procedures in 2007 were, in decreasing order, Botulinum Toxin type A, Hyaluronic Acid Fillers, and Laser Hair Removal. Many experts predict that as combination therapy becomes more popular and facial injectables more mainstream, these numbers will continue to grow and the elective pie will continue to expand. Add to this a growing recognition among aesthetic practitioners of the value of injectables as a continually replenishable profit center as well as the increasing accessibility of injectable training programs and the cosmetic boom drives on.

One of the biggest assumptions you can make as a practitioner is that you will always know what your client wants. If they come in asking for BOTOX Cosmetic to smooth fine lines and wrinkles, dig deeper into their reasoning for wanting this. There is so much information available today that we simply assume that everyone who knows the word BOTOX Cosmetic understands what it does for them. But that assumption is often wrong. When patients walk in your door looking for a way to look younger they often assume from the commercial they saw that everyone will look like the BOTOX Cosmetic model simply by having BOTOX Cosmetic injections. Begin with open ended questions. "I saw on the appointment schedule that you came in today for BOTOX Cosmetic, what specific outcome are you looking for?" If your patient tells you they want to take ten years off their appearance because they want to change careers and think they need a more youthful look, emphasize to them that this may not be accomplished with BOTOX Cosmetic alone. Instead, they may be a more ideal candidate for combination therapy personalized to meet their individual needs. An option may include recommending a medical skin care program, light laser resurfacing, and volumization. BOTOX Cosmetic would fit in perfectly with this regimen to help smooth fine lines and wrinkles and shape the face while the other modalities would provide rejuvenation on other levels. And although your client may ultimately be overwhelmed by the total package cost and associated downtime of your recommended plan, it is far better to have them walk out the door without undergoing any service than to have the expectation that BOTOX Cosmetic alone will provide them an outcome that is totally unrealistic.

As aesthetic medicine continues to change, so also does the consultation process associated with it. Although we are highly educated and highly trained physicians who may know 99% of the time what is best for the 51 year old divorcee standing in front of us, we also must keep in mind that we are competing with many other core and non-core practitioners who may ultimately offer the same services. As previously discussed, our clients determine what value is…not us. Today's consultation should involve putting a prospective client in front of a mirror and asking them if they could choose to have any part of their face or body be different what would it be and how would it change. Let them tell you what they see but guide them carefully through this process. When they are done remarking that they want smaller facial pores, softening of wrinkles around their eyes, tighter skin to their neck, less droopy eyelids, and improvement of their hands to match the age of their face and neck, your job is to layout the process of how all that will get done and how great they will look when it is finished. The commercial that will run in their heads will be; total aesthetic makeover $25,000, meeting and dating that new man of your dreams who is 10 years younger; priceless. In the long run, the cost will be easier for them to accept because you didn't talk them into these procedures…they did. With all of the training we have for procedures, never overlook the need for continued improvement on the actual consultation process itself. By staying current on effective communication skills, you will insure that you are meeting the needs of your clients and maximizing the profitable growth of your business.

CHAPTER SUMMARY POINTS:

- Patients are not only looking for improvement, they are also looking for prevention.

- The highest amount growth is occurring in the area of minimally invasive procedures. Be educated and be prepared to offer these treatments for continued growth.

- More important than talking to your patients is actually listening to your patients

Chapter 4

POTENTIAL GROWTH, DEMOGRAPHICS, AND FUTURE TRENDS

*"Success is going from failure to failure
without losing your enthusiasm."*

Abraham Lincoln

To illustrate the effectiveness of cosmetic surgery and its potential for restorative effects far beyond the physical, a recent headline loudly declared, "Unemployed? Get a Face Lift". Current economic conditions have underscored the competitive nature of the American workplace and the importance (whether we like it or not) of looking our very best. Add to this a number of studies that have clearly documented the importance of physical appearance and directly correlated it to the degree of competitiveness and ability to not only get a job, but also to keep that job. So with that in mind, let's look at these effects under current economic conditions.

While more expensive (and invasive) surgical procedures have recently dropped in popularity, injectables have shown less of a change. With it, use of BOTOX Cosmetic has continued to grow as busy executives increasingly rely on shorter downtime procedures to help them enhance their appearance.

One recent study by Dr. Liu, et al in the June 2008 issue of Plastic & Reconstructive Surgery dramatically underscored the tremendous growth potential for cosmetic enhancement. The authors analyzed annual US

Cosmetic surgery procedure volume as reported by the American Society of Plastic Surgeons (ASPS) National Clearinghouse of Plastic Surgery statistics between 1992 and 2005 and focused on the ability of economic and noneconomic variables to predict annual cosmetic surgery volume. They also relied on growth rate analyses to construct models to predict future growth and suggest trends. And they found the following.

The authors concluded that none of the economic and noneconomic variables were a significant predictor of annual surgery volume. Instead, basing their predictions on current compound annual growth rates, they concluded that by the year 2015, both surgical and nonsurgical volumes will exceed 55 million procedures per year. They projected that ASPS members alone will perform 299 surgical and 2165 nonsurgical procedures per year while non-ASPS members will annually perform 39 surgical and 1448 nonsurgical procedures. Most importantly, they concluded that if current growth rates continue over the next decade, future demand for cosmetic surgery will be largely driven by non-surgical procedures.

With these predictions comes awareness that with increasing demand, there will be an increasing need for training and education to assure optimal and reliable outcomes. While the authors predict that a majority of this demand will be met by core Plastic Surgeons, they also point to the potential for a growing contingent of non-core providers prepared to meet this demand. As such, not only will the provider need to be adequately prepared to provide effective outcomes (via training and education) but so also will the consumer need to be educated as to whom they should trust to meet their cosmetic enhancement needs. As I have always emphasized to my clients, technology is only as effective as the provider behind it. There are no miracle treatments and good results are the combination of both what is being used and who is doing it. But despite this, commoditization as a means of competition will inevitability grow in popularity as patients seek out bargain providers to meet their needs. As such, education of our target audience as to realistic expectations will become increasingly critical in helping to assure acceptable outcomes across the board. Transparency in provider training and education will likely become the norm as state medical boards seek to more adequately educate this consumer on just who is doing what and, more importantly, if they should even be doing it.

And to that end, our clients are not only seeking less invasive procedures, they are also talking about them. A recent study by the Aesthetic Surgery Education & Research Foundation (ASERF) queried 687 facial injectable patients and found some interesting information. Of those responding, 87 percent (nearly 9 out of 10) said that they openly discuss their BOTOX Cosmetic and HA dermal filler treatments with others. The study also revealed that the average facial injectable patient is a married, working mother between 41-65 years of age with a household income of $100,000. The study also pointed to that fact that these patients are health-conscious and philanthropy-minded with the majority being avid exercisers (78%) and almost a third actively volunteering with charitable organizations (32%).

And so with this in mind, we now turn to the latest facts and figures. According to the American Society of Aesthetic Plastic Surgeons (ASAPS), over ten million surgical and nonsurgical cosmetic procedures were performed in the United States in 2008. Although this number in itself is dramatic, the numbers are even more impressive and yield more truths if we break them down further.

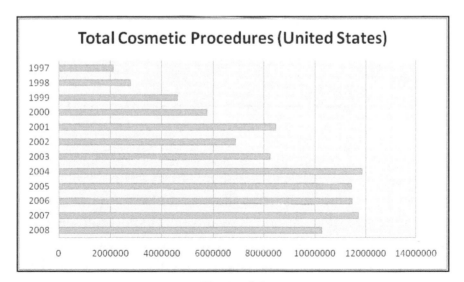

Figure 4.1

As Figure 4.1 demonstrates, the field of Aesthetic Medicine saw dramatic growth from the period of 1997-2008. And while the overall number of procedures (surgical + non-surgical) contracted a bit around 2007, the relative increase as compared to the 1997 was significant.

Breaking down these numbers a bit more in Figure 4.2, we now look at the difference between surgical and non-surgical procedures during this same procedure. And this is where we identify the real change in this industry. While growth overall during this ten year period was substantial, the real growth occurred within the non-surgical procedures as the aging population sought out ways in which to look refreshed...but with minimal downtime and potentially with less financial outlay.

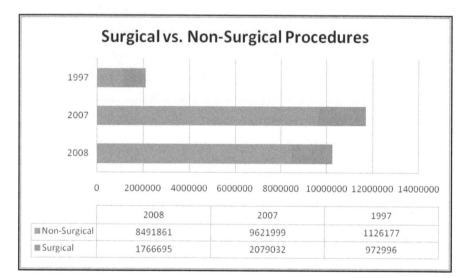

Figure 4.2

During this period, while surgical procedures increased by almost 80%, nonsurgical procedures increased by just over 233%. And as previously stated, in the following year (2008) total cosmetic procedures performed rose to just over 10 million. As Figure 4.3 so clearly shows, this number showed continued dominance in the non-surgical arm (surgical = 17% vs. non-surgical = 83%).

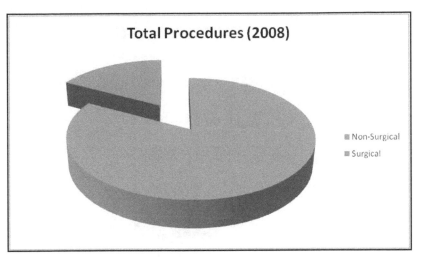

Figure 4.3

Analyzing these trends further, we now look at what was actually being done. In 2008, the top surgical procedures overall included abdominoplasty, rhinoplasty, eyelid surgery, liposuction, and breast augmentation (**Figure 4.4**) while the predominant non-surgical procedures included BOTOX Cosmetic injections, Laser Hair Removal, Hyaluronic Acid Filler injections, and Laser Skin Resurfacing (**Figure 4.5**)

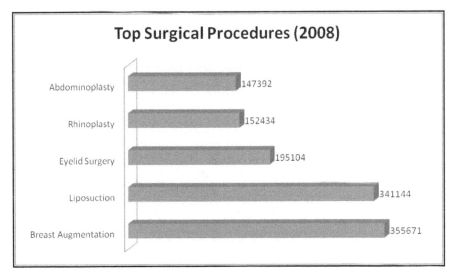

Figure 4.4

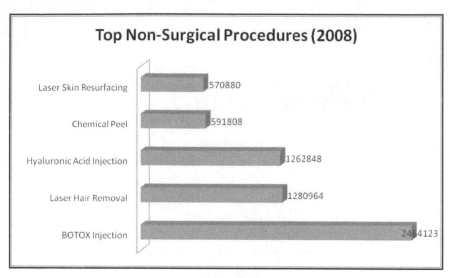

Figure 4.5

In 2008, women underwent over 9.3 million cosmetic procedures or almost 92% of total procedures performed. And as **Figure 4.6** illustrates, predominant areas of focus were localized to breast enhancement and body contouring.

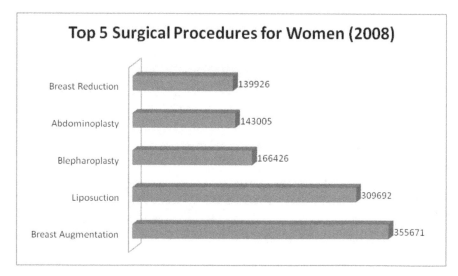

Figure 4.6

Men, on the other hand, underwent over 800,000 procedures and their areas of concentration focused more on body contouring and facial rejuvenation (FIGURE 4.7).

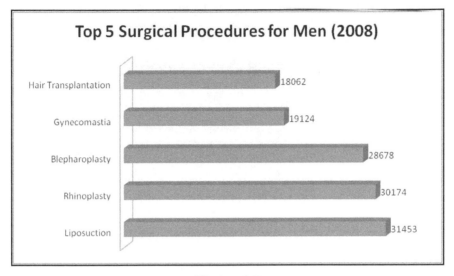

Figure 4.7

Now that know that women are the predominant participants in this field, let's look at specific age groups. As FIGURE **4.8** demonstrates, the greatest utilization of cosmetic procedures occurred within those of 35-50 years of age. Why is this important? This critical information tells us the biggest slice of pie that we potentially could benefit from and the area in which we will most likely have the best success.

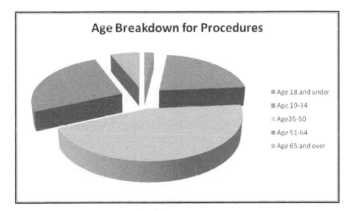

Figure 4.8

Analyzing this data further, we can now target specific age groups and identify what they were actually having done (both surgically as well as non-surgically). Turning first to the surgical procedures, we find that that the youngest patients (18 years of age and under), concentrated their focus on reshaping of the nose, ears, and breast.

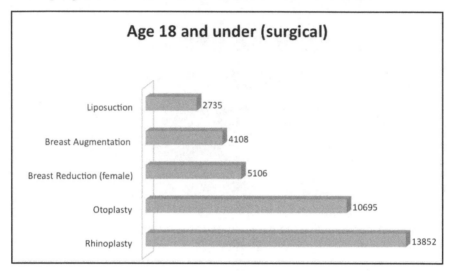

Figure 4.9

The next age group (19-34 years of age) concentrated more on breast enhancement and body contouring followed by nasal reshaping (FIGURE 4.10)

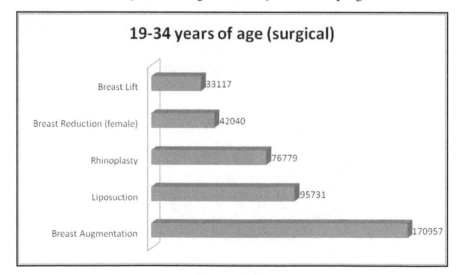

Figure 4.10

The largest group, those 35-50 years of age, remained focused on breast enhancement and body contouring (FIGURE 4.11).

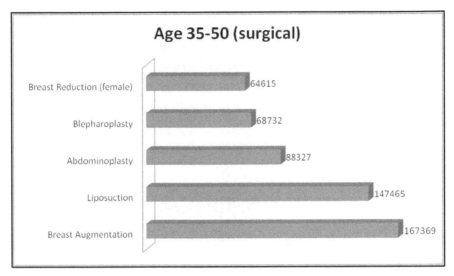

Figure 4.11

But as Figure 4.12 illustrates, the next group directed their efforts at facial rejuvenation followed by body contouring.

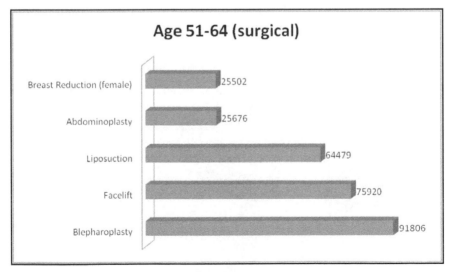

Figure 4.12

And finally, those 65 and over were almost exclusively interested in facial rejuvenation with the next area of interest being body contouring (Figure 4.13).

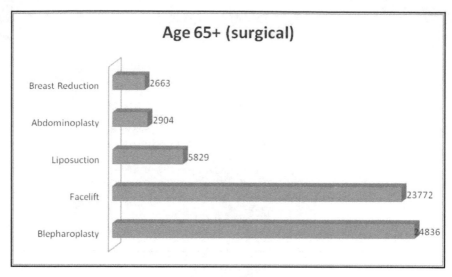

Figure 4.13

As a side note, since breast augmentation has become so popular, we should also understand specifically why patients are seeking out this enhancement.

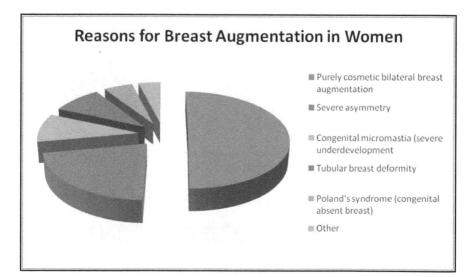

Figure 4.14

Looking at non-surgical procedures, we find that those 18 years and younger were most interested in laser hair removal followed by chemical peels and microdermabrasion (Figure 4.15).

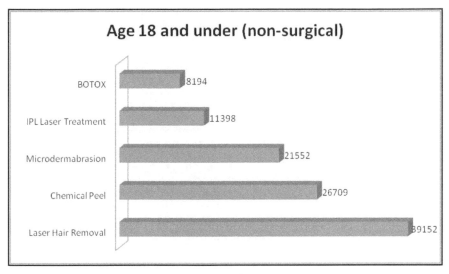

Figure 4.15

The top procedure for the next age group, 19-34 years of age, was still laser hair removal but then the focus switched to BOTOX Cosmetic and the HA fillers (Figure 4.16).

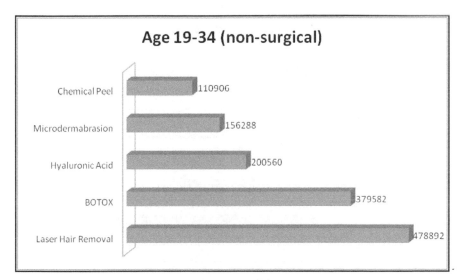

Figure 4.16

And in the next age group (35-50 years of age), BOTOX Cosmetic and the facial injectables clearly outweighed all other procedures with laser hair removal dropping into a close third place in popularity (Figure 4.17).

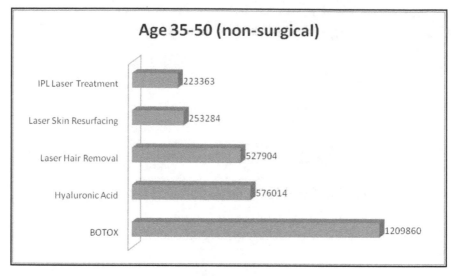

Figure 1.17

In the 51-64 year old group, this same pattern predominated (**Figure 4.18**) and even carried through to the last group (**Figure 4.19**).

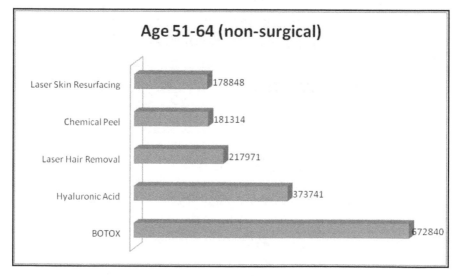

Figure 4.18

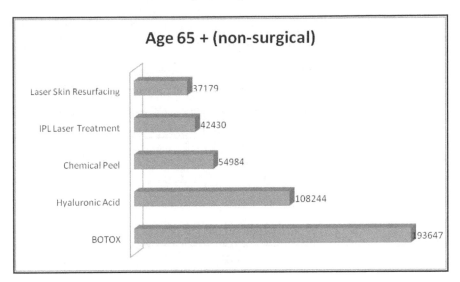

Figure 4.19

Although Caucasians remain the dominant users of both surgical and non-surgical aesthetic services, growth is being seen more and more in the non-Caucasian population. As **Figure 4.20** depicts, the largest group is the Hispanic population followed closely by the African-American segment and the Asians.

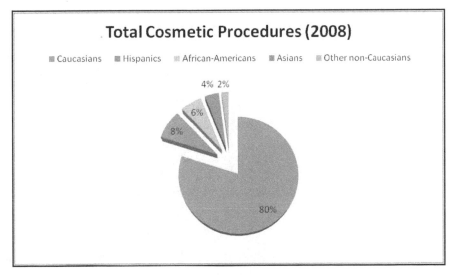

Figure 4.20

Now that we better understand who was doing what, let's look at where these procedures were actually being performed. Because a large percentage of these procedures were non-surgical, the majority were ultimately performed in an office setting (**Figure 20.1**). From here, the next category was the free standing surgery center and then the hospital. Explosive growth of the surgery center during the last ten years was most likely driven by an interest, on the part of the practitioner, for more control over both cost as well as time in addition to a more stylized and spa-like appearance for their aesthetic patient.

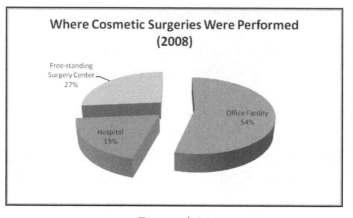

Figure 4.21

According to ASAPS, in their 2008 survey percent of practitioners polled said that they did not offer "spa" services (e.g. wraps, facials, massages) in conjunction with their medical practices and 86 percent say they did not work in conjunction with medical spas where nonsurgical procedures, such as injections and laser procedures were being performed.

Given the fact that Americans alone spent almost $11.8 billion on cosmetic procedures in 2008, the quick response would be that there is generally very good acceptance across the board for elective procedures. But is necessarily the case? According to the ASAPS poll, 62% of women and 51% of men said that they approved of cosmetic surgery. And of these, 40% of women but only 18% of men said that they would consider cosmetic surgery for themselves now, or in the future. This obviously leaves a great deal of room for growth in the coming years. But although the number of both men and women considering cosmetic surgery (according to this poll) may seem low, 73% of women and 69% of men admitted that if they did undergo cosmetic surgery in the future, they would not be embarrassed if people outside their immediate family and close friends knew about it.

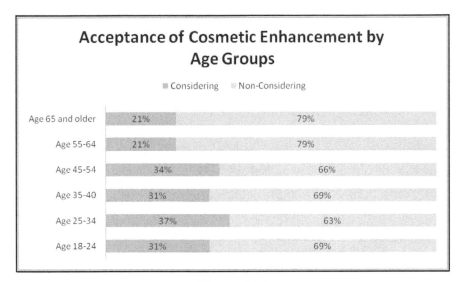

Figure 4.22

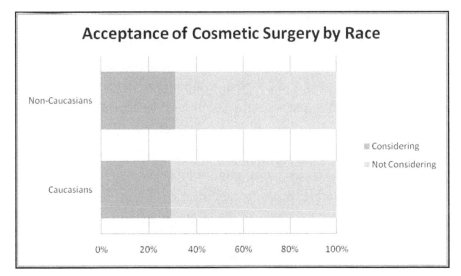

Figure 4.23

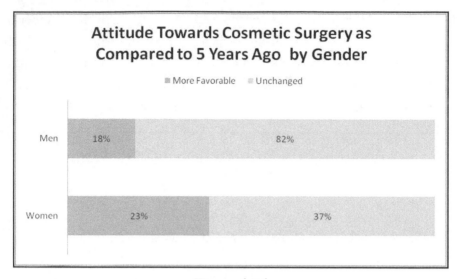

Figure 4.24

What these numbers represent is that fact that while cosmetic enhancement has dramatically increased over the last ten years, the field itself still has a long way to go to achieve complete acceptance. And while this may seem like a negative phenomenon, in reality it represents a significant opportunity for expanding the population of consumers seeking elective services. With better education of the consumer and more focused marketing, this population can theoretically be grown to numbers far out-sizing current demand. The important fact to remember is that to attract your client, you must first understand who they are in order to design a focused and coherent campaign of branding, marketing, and advertising. This concept is critical and will be discussed in depth in following chapters.

American consumers are utilizing both surgical and non-surgical procedures to look their very best and, despite economic pressures, this trend appears to be stable. But this interest in cosmetic enhancements has not gone unnoticed by our international colleagues. As demand continues to grow, supply in the form of additional providers is not surprisingly going to come not only from within the United States but also from outside our borders.

Turning our attention to the international scene, according to an article published in The Indian Journal of Post Graduate Medicine, the earliest mention of plastic surgery dates back nearly 4000 years ago in Hindu mythology when Lord Shiva seemingly performed the first plastic surgery procedure by attaching an elephant's head on the body of his son, Ashwini Kumar.

A brief 2000 years later and wound care were now being described on Egyptian papyrus hieroglyphs and flap reconstructions detailed in the Sushruta-Samhita of India. But the modern era of plastic surgery was most clearly refined during the Second World War when modern surgical innovations were applied to the treatment of battle injuries and advancements in aseptic technique and anesthesia allowed for dramatic improvements in not only outcome but also in provision for lower peri-operative morbidity.

With sweeping changes in the world economy and resultant growth of the middle class, demand for cosmetic surgery is now being seen on a worldwide basis. In India alone, prosperity in urban cities such as Mumbai, Delhi, Kolkata, Chennai, Bangalore, Pune, and Chandigarh have resulted in a growing population eager for the benefits of cosmetic enhancement. And while these procedures were previously limited to celebrities and the affluent, growing demand is now being seen among a middle class who realizes the potential for better jobs and potentially a better marriage partner.

According to a report titled, Indian Aesthetic (Cosmetic Surgery) Industry: A Primer, published by Koncept Analytics (a Delhi-based research and consulting firm), analysis of the Indian cosmetic surgery industry revealed a compound growth rate of 34% during the period 2005-2007 and estimated this micro-economy to be worth an estimated US $110 million with a majority of profits being generated from the invasive/surgical procedures. This being said, this study too identified significant current and future growth in the area of non-invasive procedures.

The report also pointed to the improving purchasing power and standard of living of the Indian populace. The Indian population represents an estimated 16.9% or 1.1 billion of overall global population. With its increasing per capita income, a report by the Economist Intelligence Unit (EIU) predicts that this will make India the 8th largest wealth center the 2017. Furthermore, according to the annual Cap Gemini/Merrill Lynch wealth report, there were 50,000 millionaires in India in 2002 and 100,000 presently. This figure alone represents 1.1% of the overall millionaires in the world.

Add to this growing internal demand for cosmetic surgery a worldwide demand for cost-effective outcomes, and a growing provider workforce within India and you have the recipe for explosive interest in cosmetic enhancement from both those within and from abroad. As such, the sector of Medical tourism has seen increasing growth as those from European countries, the Middle East, Asian and African Countries, and the United States flock to India for what they see as a cost-effective alternative.

And so with increasing supply, how do we effectively compete with and meet this challenge of medical tourism? The answer is easy. To compete, we simply need to follow the same measures we would take in competing with our colleagues within the states. The effect of commoditization and price-point setting must be offset and met head on by emphasizing a results-based practice with a strong focus on patient education. Our audience must be educated as to what they are getting and why and what they can do to achieve the best return on their investment with the least amount of risk. Quite simply, our international colleagues must be competed against in the same way that we compete within our own walls. With the understanding that growth, popularity and availability of medical tourism will continue, we need to emphasize training, experience, and outcomes as a yardstick with which to measure consumer return on investment. Our competition will ultimately emphasize price; we need to emphasize outcomes and accountability.

CHAPTER SUMMARY POINTS:

- Future growth is heavily concentrated in the area of facial injectables, lasers and other minimally invasive procedures.

- Competition will continue to growth both domestically and internationally. Be prepared and be ready to compete on a global level.

- Effective training is the most critical component for providing optimal and consistent results to your client base.

SECTION 2

STARTING DOWN THE PATH

Chapter 5

SO YOU WANT TO START AN AESTHETIC PRACTICE

"I could never convince the financiers that Disneyland was feasible because dreams offer too little collateral."

Walt Disney

So you've decided to take the first step and jump out of insurance-based medicine. Whether you are doing it all the way by jumping in head first and committing to a full-time aesthetic practice or if you are starting a bit slower and seeking just to add a few elective non-insurance based services to your current business model, let me reassure you that in doing so you've entered a field where you will finally receive more equitable reimbursement for your time and efforts than you will from insurance. In addition, by choosing this path, in the long run you will have more control over both your work hours as well as your working conditions. The biggest advantage to an elective, cash-based practice is return of control over your destiny and expansion in the possibilities for your future business and lifestyle. But do not take this step lightly, because it isn't for everyone. Although it tends to predictably lower your quality of life and consistently frustrate you, insurance based medicine is predictable and consistent and can be a stable firm hold...especially in a down economy.

Odds are you won't be taking this step by yourself. You will find the landscape filled with plenty of others who think the same way as you and who have also decided to escape the insurance rat-race. Take heart in the fact that the reason so many physicians are choosing this route is because there is so much value in doing it. Instead of running from an insurance-based business, they are effectively running toward something that can have a very positive influence on their lifestyle and practice. Having said that, never lose sight of the fact that competition and other barriers to entry in this market may initially prove daunting. To understand how best to compete and win, you first need to identify specific barriers to entry.

As you begin, you will immediately notice that there is tremendous competition for cash-paying clients. Just like you, your competitors want to build their client base as rapidly as possible with the best possible clients. To address this, you need to know how to effectively brand, market, and advertise your practice to position yourself as a key and effective player within the marketplace. Choice of branding is a very critical decision because it is very difficult, if not impossible, to change your brand once it is established. Wal-Mart, for example, is very successful as a low price retail distributor. As such, it does not compete head to head with Nordstrom's. Wal-Mart would find it difficult if not impossible to convince Nordstrom's shoppers that they have created an upgraded product line that is of the quality that Nordstrom's provides. People just wouldn't believe it. In the same manner, if you are branded as the low cost provider in your aesthetic market, your client base will rarely allow you to adjust your pricing up without losing many if not all of them. Branding is the first and crucial step in establishing your elective aesthetic practice. Without knowing how you want to position yourself, you're simply jumping back into the ineffective, big net approach. This topic will be addressed more comprehensively in its own chapter.

Next, understand that because there are so many people entering the competition, certain procedures will necessarily become commoditized. Laser hair removal is a good example of this. This procedure is often priced low enough to simply get people in the door for other goods and services. But be careful. While this "loss leader" approach may prove effective initially, in the long run it simply undervalues your services and reduces overall ROI. So while you should be sensitive to pricing variables within your local market, be careful not to compete on price alone. A better strategy would be to package laser hair removal with an upper body makeover so that you can price it at cost or better. You have to be able to determine if a product like laser hair removal or microdermabrasion, for example, contributes to getting the type of clients and associated profitable services you want. If not, don't offer it. Find a competent partner who does these procedures and refer your patient to them. In attracting the price shopper, you are filling your schedule with non-loyal warm bodies that simply jump to the next practice, med-spa, or hair salon with the latest special while losing out on the premium customer who can't get in to see you when they want because your schedule is too full.

Another effect of commoditization is that undifferentiated price competition occurs whether it is good for the market or not. A negative effect of price competition is that outcomes and quality become subordinate and price becomes the sole differentiating variable between similar products and services offered within that marketplace. You can relate healthcare pricing/cost to a 3 legged stool. One leg is access to care, a second leg is quality, and the third leg is cost. You can typically have 2 of 3 of those legs but never all three. If you want cost to be lower you either give up quality or you give up access. Access is given up if you want of cost and quality because eventually at low prices and high quality you push providers of the services out of the market because they become unprofitable and can't stay in. Be careful with how your approach affects price competition and ultimately the commoditization of a service line.

Commoditization is said to occur when the market changes from monopolistic competition to one of perfect competition. At this stage, oversupply occurs and there is essentially no differentiation that the market recognizes or will pay for. Everyone and every service is considered to be equal in value. To this, one Blogger commented as follows:

> *"So, how can it be said that consumers, not competition, are the driving force of commoditization? When consumers perceive that all products are the same, their only real factor for selecting one supplier over another becomes price. The key for every business is to not become concerned with the competition because in the end, you cannot prevent competitors from entering your market. Instead, businesses should focus on the consumer's perspective. If to the consumer you have no competition, then price is the last thing on their mind." (http://www.carterandcompanyllc. com/2008/03/avoiding-commoditization-with-hi-tech.html)*

As such, the emphasis should be placed not on keeping up with the competition but, instead, the outcome value that the patient is looking for. If you can achieve that better than your competition, you will have your choice of the premium business within your market.

Although the phenomenon of commoditization is being seen on a national level and potentially eating into profit margins and ROI, it doesn't need to. The facial injectable is a good example of a procedure that is more frequently being positioned on price alone. Within my practice, even though I am a high-volume injector, I am still subject to price pressure from competition. To secure my clients' business at a higher price-point, I emphasize the value of the extra training I receive and my team's ability to stay on the cutting edge of injectable technology. I will even show them photos of patients who have had minor to even severe problems when injected by people who don't have the same level of training and experience. I emphasize end-results with my own before and after photographs and utilize clients for word of mouth marketing and direct referrals. A fully informed patient who sees the value of training and experience along with the value of a practice that emphasizes safety will not make price their primary issue.

There are plenty of market studies available that prove that price is usually well down on a buyers list when the purchase is something personal to them. Price only rises to the top when providers fail to show a differentiated value in the product or service line. Don't fall into the trap of trying to be price-competitive with other practices who don't demonstrate your level of quality and experience. Value awareness on the part of a consumer takes time to develop and it usually happens as part of your brand. The moment you fall into the price game you lose along with everyone else. If you do 25% less volume then your competition at 40% higher prices you not only make more total profit you also have capacity to do other things because your schedule is not full of low to no margin clients. But also be careful not to price yourself out of the marketplace. In the area of facial injectables, for example, I offer reasonable pricing for several reasons. First, this is an area that I truly enjoy and I want to build and maintain volume within this area. But most importantly, I want to make sure that my patients are adequately corrected. The biggest mistake injectors make is to under-correct their patients. When they do, and they achieve a suboptimal outcome, their patient is going to advertise this result to the entire community. And when they do so, they predictably will not be telling everyone that they, the patient, elected to under-correct. Remember, each and every one of your patients is a billboard for your practice and you are only as good as your last result. With that in mind, I price my procedures to make them affordable to the right patient and try and avoid the trap of under-correction. If a patient cannot afford full correction, I will often turn them away until they can. Otherwise, I am effectively undoing all good press and sending the message that I deliver mediocre results.

As I stated above, competition within my local marketplace is a reality but I differentiate myself based upon providing an entirely different product. With facial injectables, I am no longer merely treating lines and wrinkles, I am affecting facial shaping and providing, in many cases, a non-surgical solution for a patient population not interested in going under the knife. In this way, I am stepping away from my competition because I am offering an entirely different service. As such, I am potentially reducing the impact of local commoditization on my local practice pattern.

Keep in mind that when performed correctly, facial injectables are a highly lucrative profit center and one of the most effective tools for achieving facial rejuvenation. Performed incorrectly, they can produce results that are overdone, asymmetric, unnatural, or simply incorrect.

As a national trainer and consultant for several injectable companies, I have seen a wide range of ability among both physicians and nurses. To me, the most critical variable in a good injector is an aesthetic eye. The technique of injecting these products is far less important than knowing where to actually inject them. Simply erasing lines and wrinkles is no longer considered a good outcome. An experienced injector must understand the process of facial shaping, appreciate subtle differences between various products, and be able to maximize outcome while balancing price-point and optimal correction. And while I am sensitive to my client's budget, I am also critically aware that if I under-correct, undervolumize, and effectively under-treat, I am producing a result that will tell everyone this person comes in contact with that I do deliver sub-optimal results. With respect to marketing, one bad outcome can effectively destroy every good promotional campaign and prove to be extremely expensive in the long run. As such, guide your clients to an outcome based upon your skill set and experience and do not let budget be the only determining factor in how you treat anyone.

Your practice is a business. Begin with a good business plan. Anticipate your expenditures and identify a set revenue level that will allow you to live the way you wish to live. I learned early on to let each professional do what they do best. I am a surgeon and although I understand a good amount about the legal system, I am in no way suited to act as my own attorney. The same applies to my financial matters. To that end, the money I pay each month to my attorney, my CPA, and to my money manager has not only kept me out of harm's way, but has also enabled me to grow my practice in directions I never anticipated. For example, I recently spun off a separate corporation for my consulting efforts. In doing so, this entity affords me the ability to partition related expenses more effectively which affords me less tax liability and legal exposure than if I were operating under my primary corporation. For specific details on how to structure your main entity as well as any subsidiary businesses, I encourage you to consult the expertise of a good attorney as well as a good CPA. They are worth their weight in gold and will free you up to do what you do best… be a doctor.

The same approach applies to branding, marketing, and advertising. Again, while I have a fair amount of knowledge in these three areas, I also learned early on that not only did I not have the time to manage all of this on my own but that I am not also the most effective person to manage these areas. To this end, I currently work with a Public Relations firm responsible for guiding the look and feel of my practice. This firm adjudicates the consistency of my brand and the effectiveness of new initiatives. But simply hiring a PR firm is not enough. To best utilize this resource, you again must first know where you're going, what look and feel you would like to convey, and most importantly, understand the image you wish to project to potential clients. By identifying and understanding these variables, you can help your publicist guide you in the right direction and achieve the most effective ROI.

Another variable to consider in your entrance and continued success within the aesthetic marketplace is the growing impact of changing technology. Each year, technological advances within the industry come and go with few proving to stand the test of time. The most glaring examples of this are the many lasers released each year and the few that actually remain as gold standards of care once the dust settles. While many are touted as the latest and greatest, they eventually prove to have outcomes that are often difficult to reproduce on a large scale (in other words, you the practitioner cannot achieve the same amazing results that you saw at the dinner talk where you first saw the laser promoted) or have an unacceptable degree of downtime or an unacceptable price-point.

With this comes the ever increasing importance of staying on top of new technologies and offering your patients effective strategies to address the aging process. But what is the best way to assess efficacy? Many early adopters latch onto the latest and greatest hoping to ride the wave of national marketing campaigns (generally from the companies themselves) and public interest. While this may prove effective as a short term strategy, be careful that you are not simply acquiring leases on expensive devices or purchasing products that, in the long run, may prove to be yet another proverbial flash in the pan. I have always tried to offer the latest to my clients, but I also realize that bad results early on may prove more damaging than no results at all. In other words, adopting the latest and greatest with ineffective results may do more to injure your reputation as an experienced aesthetic provider. To that end, I rely on a few tried and tested approaches.

First, I weigh who is promoting the new product/service based upon their prior credibility. I then consult with other peers as to their experience with the product. If very few people are latching onto something, it generally tells me that either everyone else is uninformed or this technology is not revolutionary. More often than not new laser technology is simply incremental improvement on old technology and not necessarily worth the extra cost of upgrading. As a buyer of technology you need to understand up front how to assess value that technology before you ever attempt to buy it or you will get burned. For example, having worked with several medical spas, I quickly learned that few lasers ever completely live up to their claims. This doesn't mean that they won't bring value to your practice. You simply need to make sure you know what that laser is good at and what it is not good at and then determine if you can live with the strengths and weaknesses of the technology in your practice.

Having said that, I recently purchased a fractional CO_2 laser. Before making this purchase, I thoroughly researched available competitors, spoke with several trusted peers, and carefully reviewed the literature to determine whether or not I felt that this would be a significant advance worthy of such a large investment. And so far it has been. However, this investment was made after turning away other similar devices which I did not feel would grant me both efficacy and good ROI on time spent. I also have the advantage of working in a group setting where the financial outlay is shared by three practitioners. For those in the solo setting, I encourage you to begin by renting such a device on a case by case basis and actually see if the results meet your standards. If they do, you can always purchase. Once you do purchase, however, you are stuck with the device…good or bad.

Whether or not you should buy or lease depends upon your present financial situation and how such a choice will impact you in the long run. Talk to your CPA about depreciation incentives, tax law, and long term financial implication and never make such a large investment without seriously evaluating it. It is a proven method to dramatically impact your practice…in a very negative way. Yet another option if you are either cash strapped or not convinced of efficacy is to outsource various procedures. For example, if you are unsure about whether to enter the injectables market, hire a nurse injector on a commission-only basis and evaluate net profitability after six months. If a true profit center has been created, roll that person into your practice. If not, you have learned a very valuable lesson…for a fraction of the cost.

In my experience, I have learned the advantages and disadvantages of being the first to market with a product or service line. While it is often tempting to offer the latest and greatest that your clients just saw on the morning news, I am careful to evaluate not only what products and services work best but also what works best for my particular client base. This is an important lesson. For example, one of the most popular national skincare lines is extremely effective at reversing facial aging…but at a price. While it often provides outstanding results long-term, in the short term many patients find the dryness, peeling, flaking, and general skin sensitivity to be unbearable. In my geographic location, these side effects are made worse by the fact that there is very little humidity to begin with and so this product tends to have an even greater, more pronounced degree of dissatisfaction than more humid regions. Don't focus on what works best, focus on what works best for your clients.

CHAPTER SUMMARY POINTS:

- More important than increased revenue is the fact that an aesthetic practice can give you back control over your own schedule and quality of life.

- Branding is critical for distinguishing you from the rest of the herd.

- Be prepared to address commoditization of your products and services.

- Start with a good business plan.

- Hire the right people. You simply cannot do everything well.

Chapter 6

FEATURES OF THE NEW MEDICAL PRACTICE

"Winning is not a sometime thing. You don't win once in a while, you don't do things right once in a while, you do them right all the time. Winning is a habit. Unfortunately, so is losing."

Vincent Lombardi

A question commonly asked by a marketing consultant is "What is your market area?" The new medical practice has to be defined differently from those built in the past. And with that, the definition of market area and services offered has clearly changed. With increasing connectivity, new practices find themselves operating not only locally but potentially globally as the internet continues to break down boundaries and extends the reach of your practice. The practice also has to consider new technology and the opportunities and problems that can come with it. Tele-consulting is a phenomenon which began several years ago but has only recently been embraced by the medical profession. This type of business model has proven extremely useful in extending consultative medical care to smaller rural communities which are potentially underserved by medical services. If you live in an area such as Denver, Colorado, tele-consultation to mountain town communities can yield nice results for your business with just two or three referrals.

Wikipedia, the online dictionary used to define popular culture, describes "tele-presence" as "the set of technologies which allow a person to feel as if they were present, to give the appearance that they were present, or to have an effect, at a location other than their true location." Although tele-presence functions—teleconferencing and telecommuting—were originally developed for non-medical applications, in time they may prove to be an effective means for long range consulting with new or existing clients in a means greatly expanded beyond the conventional phone call or email. While potential for this application is currently limited by equipment costs, over time this may prove to be an effective means for expanding patient base to out-of-town clients. One scenario may proceed as follows. A patient in Arkansas calls to inquire about breast augmentation from a Plastic Surgeon in Los Angeles. This potential client is then directed to a local tele-presence facility—equipped with audio, video, and high bandwidth connection—and a live consultation takes place even though the two, or more, participants, are in different locations. With continued adoption of broadband technology and settling of the price-point., I'm convinced that in the future this technology will play a large role in how we run our practices.

With increased connectivity via the internet your marketing reach to these underserved areas previously untapped by conventional marketing methods can be very inexpensive (often pennies on the dollar as compared to conventional marketing approaches). Another more local application of this technology would be to have a web page, one of typically 10- 20 pages within your website, added to your site that is optimized for a small town. This can be done very easily. If you have a Denver-based practice and you added one page on your website dedicated to Durango, Colorado (a small town in rural Colorado) it would cost you virtually nothing. But when Durango residents are looking for aesthetic solutions on the internet, your web page will come at or near the top and you can emphasize an ability to do consulting over a video connection and then have them make a trip to your office for treatment. One client a month from any of several underserved small towns around your market area will more than pay for cost of the tele-presence and you can start referral programs in these small towns after a single successful patient experience.

But while telemedicine is years away from widespread adoption, web conferencing is rapidly gaining acceptance within the medical community. This technology allows multiple participants to participate in live meetings or simply view presentations over the Internet which can also be used very effectively for training. With each person connected to the conference via a downloaded software application. During the presentation, multiple options for conducting the meeting can be chosen. One type of teleconferencing, the "webinar," is generally a one-way presentation in which a speaker presents a slide presentation (generally with audio). During the presentation, the audience (anyone connected to the webinar) may type in questions (through the CHAT option) or call in to a central number to verbally ask questions. To enable this interaction, webinars are most commonly performed live and then recorded and archived for viewing later, a convenience when people want to participate later, say at midnight, or in another time zone. The pharmaceutical and medical device industry is rapidly latching onto this technology as a means to promote their products to a national audience at a far lower cost.

Dollar for dollar, this technology is an extremely effective technology as compared to the traditional local dinner programs. First, dinner programs can only accommodate a certain number of people due to space constraints. Next, there are costs associated with each additional participant. Finally, the contents of interaction can only be experienced live. In contrast, the webinar has fixed costs which do not increase with additional members, it has no limit to number of participants, it has national (and potentially international) reach, and it can be recorded and archived for future playback. For these reasons, webinars are rapidly gaining in popularity as a means to promote and educate the end user in many different subjects.

But how does this apply to your medical practice? Webinars can actually be a very important way in which to reach your clientele. As more and more households are adopting broadband connections, fast download speeds are becoming the norm. This means that the end consumer can actually participate, or at least view, these seminars without losing their connection or compromising on quality of video playback. Say, for example, you have a new laser that you wish to promote. One option is to have an open house during which you give a presentation on the benefits of this device, possibly fire up the laser, and then actually show what it does. Although this is the more common way to promote your services, there are several limitations.

First, not everyone has an open schedule and can attend the exact night or time you have chosen for the seminar. Next, after a long day at work, or after watching the kids all day, many clients may simply not want to leave their house. Or, something may come up that prevents them from attending that evening. A webinar gets around these limitations. Your potential client can sit in the comfort of their home and watch the webinar either live or as an archived broadcast. For those that watch the recorded broadcast, you can provide the option of emailing questions to you about this exciting new technology. In addition, many potential clients are afraid of actually attending these seminars because of privacy issues. Webinars get around this since all participants remain anonymous to anyone but the host.

My prediction is that as our lives become busier and busier, and gas prices continue to rise, web-based promotions will become more popular as a means to reach your target audience. In my practice, I see clients from several neighboring states and so being able to reach out to them without them ever having to leave their house is a very enticing means of communicating. And while the costs of maintaining a webinar site can seem a bit steep, keep in mind that the potential outreach can be dramatic. One consideration is shared webinar sites, aligning with similar practices to both lower your overall monthly expenditure as well as create synergistic marketing efforts. For example, a Plastic Surgery practice could offer webinar services along with a Cosmetic Dentist, a Lasik Surgeon, and a Dermatologist. While there may be a small amount of overlap, the advantages of lowered costs and the ability to market to clients of the combined practices can potentially outweigh any disadvantages.

In addition to challenges associated with the new technology, aesthetic practices must also be able to effectively identify and work with changing client dynamics. For several reasons, the new client is much different than the client of twenty years ago. Cosmetic enhancement has become more commonplace as a result of heightened media attention in addition to television shows directly touting the entire industry. In addition, as financing has become more readily available, services and procedures have become embraced and sought after by a wider patient base from the standpoint of socioeconomics, ethnicity, geography, and age. In addition, whereas the industry was previously almost exclusively directed to a female audience, more and more men are now participating. The result is that while competition among providers has increased (effectively slicing up the pie into smaller pieces) so also has the size of the pie. The end result is a robust industry which, if you position your practice correctly with the proper branding, marketing, and advertising, can provide substantial returns in the years to come.

While most practitioners understand the notion of yearly net revenue growth, I am surprised by how many do not evaluate ROI per procedure. This is critical. Working hard is not the goal; working effectively and optimally is. A key feature of the successful practice is a clear understanding of which products and services provide the best return. If your appointment book is full but you're merely breaking even, something is obviously wrong. In my practice, I have reduced the number of surgical procedures that I perform down to the five most profit-effective. These are the procedures that bring me the best net profit per unit time. In addition to increasing my overall profitability, narrowing my focus has also allowed me to more effectively market myself and my practice.

To further enhance my practice, I have identified a number of profit centers which not only enhance procedures that I currently perform but which are also effective revenue streams. These include a medical skincare department and nurse injectors. Consider the following statement:

"I would rather have 1% of 100 people's efforts than 100% of my own"
J. Paul Getty

So what exactly does he mean? Getty refers to the multiplier effect of leveraging talent. No matter who you are or what you do, you can only do so much. But if you add the right people and they do something from which you gain a net profit, you then have a profit center with a multiplier effect. These profit centers effectively allow you to leverage someone else's time and efforts to earn to passive income for yourself. This principle applies perfectly to the aesthetic industry where physician extenders can effectively run and become profit centers under your guidance. While you are doing what you like to do best (whether it is invasive or non-invasive procedures or even consulting), your profit centers allow you to increase the size of your pie.

But be careful. Keep in mind the idea of guilt by association. Whatever your extenders do and whatever outcomes they achieve, everything will be linked to your name. Adding the wrong people can drive up revenues in the short term; in the long run, they can potentially tarnish your reputation and even drive down your business.

In *"Good to Great,"* best-selling author Jim Collins refutes the notion the "people are your most important asset." Instead, he suggests that "the right people are." He argues that the most critical decision in building and running your company is choosing the right people and then getting out of their way and letting them do what they do best. He feels that the greatest of business plans are doomed to failure if you don't have the "right people on the bus." As such, the first step in developing any profit center is the choice of employees within it. Choose correctly, and the profit center, whatever it is, can lead to great success. Choose the wrong people and your time will be spent micro-managing their efforts, hiring and firing, and cleaning up their messes.

Another key lesson that I learned is to let professionals do what they do best and get out of their way. While I know a little about the legal system, there is no way that I want to represent myself or manage my own legal issues. That is why I have a good attorney. The same goes for my CPA and for my two publicists. My recommendation is that you do the same. While you can probably save a little money early on by personally managing branding, marketing, and advertising efforts, you will quickly learn that not only is this not your forte but that your time is better spent doing what you do best…being a doctor. While I sometimes cringe at the amount of money I spend paying consultants each year, I also recognize that I cannot do everything well and that my practice is probably much farther ahead at this point because of their combined efforts.

Emergence of the new medical practice has called into question conventional notions of what it means to practice medicine in general. This paradigm shift has changed the perspective of new physicians from one of "how and where can I serve" to "how can medicine as a profession serve me". Younger physicians are no longer willing to work long hours without equitable compensation, no longer willing to compromise their lifestyle, and they no longer see medicine as an all-encompassing career to the detriment of everything else in their lives. For too long, they have seen the high divorce rates, broken families and unacceptable levels of stress and are challenging the idea of what it actually means to be a doctor. Most importantly, they realize the need for a more balanced lifestyle in which medicine can play a role and that playing doctor does not mean sacrificing everything else that is important.

This shift in priorities is increasing the supply of doctors who wish to practice elective aesthetics because it offers them the ability to be a high quality doctor and still live with a lifestyle that suits them and their families. What does this mean for you if you choose the elective aesthetics market? You need to be outstanding to deal with the continuous stream of new competition, outstanding at delivering quality products and services, and outstanding at delivering value to the client base you establish. You must also be outstanding at retaining clients through your ability to build relationships with them that go beyond the basic client/service provider use of the internet, value based interactions when they are in your office, and the use of technology like webinars and a tele-presence when needed. The rewards are there for those who setup their medical practice in a client centric fashion with outstanding staff and go out and get business rather than waiting for it to walk in the door.

CHAPTER SUMMARY POINTS:

- Know your market but grow your practice by thinking outside this local market.

- Your client demographics are changing. Identify and be able to work with these changing dynamics.

- Working hard is not the goal. Success lies in working smart, delegating, and leveraging available talent.

- When adding staff or physician extenders, always keep in mind that there is guilt by association.

- The medical profession has changed and many practitioners with it. Be prepared to understand and embrace a completely different mindset.

Chapter 7

BENCHMARKS OF A SUCCESSFUL PRACTICE

"Whenever you see a successful business, someone once made a courageous decision."

Peter Drucker

So what actually makes a successful practice successful? To answer this, we need to look at the basics of a practice. A practice is like a relationship; once started, it must be nurtured, maintained, and grown; otherwise, it risks stagnation and failure. This is particularly true for the aesthetic practice.

The first step is constructing a successful practice is attraction. Clients must be attracted. But to identify potential clients, you first must know exactly who it is that you are going after. To reach them, you must know their habits and you must know where they go. And when you do, you must offer a solution to their problem…whatever it is. If they are concerned about facial aging, you must position yourself as the best solution for facial aging. If their concerns are saggy breasts, then you are the best solution for that. And so on. All clients come to you with a problem; your task is to help them fix it and fix it better than anyone else. And to get them in the door, you must be prepared to tell them why you are the only one that can help them.

Once you've attracted a client, the next step is to convert them. And to do so, education is essential. As compared to years ago, information about cosmetic procedures is now readily available on the internet. Add to this an increased willingness of clients to openly discuss their procedures and outcomes and you have a more savvy, educated patient population overall. But this education can also be a double-edged sword. While your clients may come in armed with information, not all of it may be accurate. At times, you may find yourself effectively un-educating your clients when they present with information that is not only inaccurate but completely wrong. A good example of this is the internet myth which states that breast implants must be replaced every ten years. As every aesthetic practitioner knows, while breast implants have a finite lifespan, they certainly do not need to be replaced on schedule in a manner similar to rotating your tires. If they fail, you replace them; if they're okay…you don't. Education should begin before the client walks through your doors and can be accomplished in a variety of ways. Your website is an excellent source of information. It can not only promote the latest and greatest procedures you are offering but, in doing so, and with the precise inclusion of keywords specific to the procedure, can also act as a means for site optimization and effectively increase organic ranking of your site. Another option for pre-education can involve either mailing or emailing procedure-specific information to your clients before their initial appointment. This makes a tremendous amount of sense and can actually save you time in the initial consultation; but only if your patients take the time to read the information.

But education doesn't stop here. Every one of your staff should know what you do and how you do it better than your competition. This is essential. When a prospective client calls your office, your staff should be able to describe basics of everything included on your menu of products and services. And, they should be able to describe your accolades in detail and know why it is that you are the proverbial best person for the job. To better educate my staff, I offer regular training meetings during which I review the latest and greatest of our offerings and make sure that they are as knowledgeable as possible. And I take this one step further. I openly encourage each and every one of my staff to experience what I do by offering them complimentary facial injectables and a free surgical procedure after they have worked with me for at least one year. In addition, they purchase medical skin care products at cost and receive chemical peels and facials from my aesthetician as their schedules permit. By doing this, I have literally created walking billboards for my work. The amount of money that I have supposedly lost by giving away facial injectables has been more than made up in referrals from clients who see the fresh, rejuvenated faces of my staff when they walk through the front door of my office. Interestingly, not all practices agree with me on this. In the past I have had the opportunity to work with medical spas and find that many spa owners are not in agreement with me on this policy. I even had one owner recently who went as far as to actually charge full price to his employees. For many reasons, I am no longer with this particular facility and, interestingly, they will probably not be in business for much longer. I find that skimping on areas such as this can have a far reaching negative effect on the entire practice. Imagine walking into your dentist's office and the receptionist has yellow teeth. This simple image would most likely color (no pun intended) your perception of this entire practice in a single moment. Keep in mind that you educate consumers on multiple levels...many of which are non-verbal but equally as powerful. Control the education process as best as possible and filter any erroneous information out as best as you can.

Results demonstrated by your staff should speak volumes about your talent. Along the same lines, each and every product offering should be backed by results in some way or another. When I speak with patients, I use my own before and after results whenever possible. If I am using a new technology (for example, a new laser treatment) for which I do not have my own results yet, I point this out to the patient. And I recruit my own patients as testimonials. This is extremely powerful! To better educate my clients, I offer each and every one of them the opportunity to speak with a patient who has actually undergone the procedure. I do not coach my patients as to what they should say. I only emphasize that they be honest with results, downtime, discomfort, and so forth. Prospective patients are not stupid and can see through scripts and templated testimonials. Don't speak down to them in this way; it will generally backfire! And remove the magazines from your waiting room. If your clients have to wait for you (and they shouldn't have to wait long), their time should be spent learning about products and services you offer and glancing through your photo brag books. The same applies to your exam rooms. I have replaced magazines in these rooms with electronic photo frames which continuously run digitized before/after loops of my results. Every opportunity you miss at educating your clients is a lost opportunity and could potentially affect their decision to move forward. Keep this in mind because the small details make all of the difference.

Now that the potential client has made it to your practice, do everything you can (within reason) to win them over. The initial consultation is an integral part of the entire process but is, unfortunately, sometimes not given as much weight as it should. The first encounter is a chance for the potential patient to be educated. More importantly, it is a chance for them to see if they are comfortable with you and if you are comfortable with them. The first step is to actually listen to your client. And while this may sound basic, not everyone does. You would be surprised what patients tell you both verbally as well as non-verbally. And when you listen, make sure and identify their key concerns. Have them list them for you in descending order of importance and identify just how comprehensively they want that concern addressed and how dramatic a change they want to achieve. Finally, structure a treatment plan based upon their individual goals, finances, and desired downtime.

And refer to your patients as "clients". Although this may sound a bit cold and certainly "un-medical", it is an important departure from the austere clinical nature of most practices and can help you move forward with them in a manner more suitable to an aesthetic practice.

Now that you have examined your client and educated them as to their options, it is time to hand them over to your "closer". This person is ultimately responsible for answering any additional questions and effectively closing the deal. At this point, an estimate should be presented to the client. Price-point should be attainable but not unreasonable. You should never be the cheapest nor should you be the most expensive. And don't be afraid to charge more than some of your competition; just be able to defend why.

CHAPTER SUMMARY POINTS:

- To convert your client, you must first know your client.

- Listen to what your client is saying and not saying. And always be attuned to non-verbal clues.

- Your staff is an extension of you—good or bad. Never forget that.

SECTION 3

INTRODUCTION OF THE FRAMEWORK

Chapter 8

THE FRAMEWORK FOR SUCCESS

"If you work just for money, you'll never make it.
But if you love what you are doing, and always
put the customer first, success will be yours."

Ray Kroc

A ll successful businesses are built around a framework. A framework is a series of related concepts and processes that define your strategy and allow you to execute the steps necessary for success. As the book unfolds, we will explore a number of concepts related to marketing, branding, and the Zone of Client Opportunity which you can then use to assemble your own business framework. In this section, we will discuss the framework itself and highlight important information pertaining to the profitable business zone.

In the most basic terms, a framework is a structure that supports something. In this case, we are talking about a framework that will support an aesthetic practice. Awareness of how the individual areas of marketing, branding, and executing in the Zone of Client Opportunity all interact is very important in driving you towards a continuously sustainable profitable business model. Understanding your framework and the interacting strategies within it is only part of the picture. In addition to this, you will also need very a set of well executed processes to support them. This factor itself is so important that if you read this section and you don't understand what we are trying to convey to you, we encourage you to stop reading this book and contact either of us for further clarification. As stated in the opening of this section there are four distinct critical areas of focus within this framework:

- **Your Market**
- **Your Brand**
- **Zone of Client Opportunity**
- **Zone of the Continuously Growing and Profitable Business**

In the next several chapters, we will identify and discuss specific components that together comprise critical concepts and processes that allow for both short and long-term success. We will also discuss how they interact with each other. An example of this may include how an individual customer's experience interacts with your marketing. Another important concept is the notion of how your consultations reflect the look and feel of your marketing efforts and brand identity. Other examples include how your brand identity moves people from the general market into your Zone of Client Opportunity as well as how your marketing, branding, and consultations help drive business into your continuously growing and profitable business. Properly executed, your practice framework assures that decisions in each critical area are aligned with your strategic business plan. It also provides an outline for execution. Never forget that strategy without execution is dreaming and execution without strategy is simply wandering. We don't want you to do either.

The framework depicted in **Figure 8.1** shows you the various marketing concepts you can use that will be discussed in later chapters. This framework begins with the process of defining and identifying your market and then follows with execution of various strategies such as website marketing, referral based marketing, and traditional marketing concepts. Even though we believe all of these different marketing concepts fit into the framework we also realize that you will gradually move through these various options and ultimately figure out which work best for you. In regards to your strategy and framework, the most important thing to remember is to specifically measure how successful each individual marketing strategy is in moving people into the Zone of Client Opportunity.

Figure 8.1

Think of it like a funnel. Your marketing strategies move people from the wider general market to the top of your funnel. All eight different strategies can be then used to drive potential clients into the top of your funnel. Once they are here, you want certain clients (see **Figure 8.2** below) to fall through into your Zone of Client Opportunity and certain ones not to. Many people ask why you wouldn't want all potential clients to go into your Zone of Client Opportunity and then be filtered out there. The reason that you want the filter process to start at the top of the funnel is that it ultimately costs you money. When they walk in your office, when you spend time with them in a consultation, and when your staff sends them information it ultimately costs you money. The more time and money you can avoid spending on potential clients who don't fit your business strategy, the more you will have for the ones you do want.

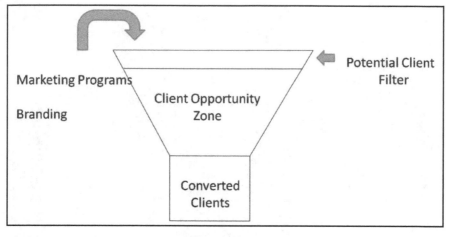

Figure 8.2

But sometimes it is difficult to identify who you don't want. The non-optimal client may find you in the same way that an optimal client would. But in your early interactions with them, it may become glaringly clear that they are simply not a good fit for you or vice-versa. And this poor fit may be the result of a number of variables. They may be a shopper and drive you crazy as they bargain shop your menu of services, they may be body dysmorphic and ultimately never satisfied with their outcome, or they may simply require way too much maintenance for you to be profitable in their care. Many times you know from the first interaction you have with these clients that they are simply not a good fit. My recommendation is to always go with your gut instincts. Weed these people out before you try and turn them from opportunity to client. In the long run, you will not only be more profitable, you will also be much happier.

The filter at the top of the funnel must be applied by knowledgeable staff or by you personally. In building your practice, you will inevitably spend a great deal of time and money training your staff to recognize opportunity and to capture potential clients. And it won't be in their minds to actually turn away people. So manage this process very carefully. Someone who wants BOTOX Cosmetic but who will only buy it from you at $6 per unit isn't worth having in your practice. Educate your clients as to why they should pay your price based on your reputation and the overall value of your practice. A shopper who knows the cost per unit of BOTOX Cosmetic and is only interested in paying you a meager amount over this cost will ultimately end up being more pain then profit. These people will negotiate a lower than market price and then proceed to tell all their friends. By allowing this, you are not only cutting your gross margins, you are also letting the general public know that you are a discount provider and ultimately sending the message that your time is worth less than the rest of your competition. We are not suggesting that this filtering process is easy; it requires that you have experience to execute it properly. You must have a high level of awareness as you process people into the Zone of Client Opportunity and improve that process over time as you gain more knowledge not only about your local market but also the specific direction in which you are driving your organization.

Once you drive someone into the Zone of Client Opportunity, you need outstanding execution by you and your staff to insure your ultimate success. Ask yourself whether you really want to capture everyone you see during a consultation, you talk on the phone with, or send information to. We would say no. What you do want is the opportunity to convert all of those you do want. Most medical practices and medical day spas train their staff on effective interaction with clients. But the most highly trained staff must still understand the process they need to go through to convert clients even with this training. For example, the standard process may involve an initial consultation, a follow-up letter or email within a day of the consultation, and a phone call inside of the first week. That process must be executed every single time. We have seen too many instances in which the email or phone call is either made very late or not made at all. Track every single client in the opportunity zone on a spread sheet or in a business software program and make sure that this process is properly executed. In addition, schedule a regular 30 minute meeting weekly with your staff to review the number of people in the Zone of Client Opportunity this week, how many did you actually convert, whether there was appropriate follow-up and execution for those not yet converted, as well as to review details of potential clients from the previous week, the previous month, or for other outliers who were still considered potential clients.

Some clients will be in the Zone of Client Opportunity for a very short period of time (perhaps a week or less) while others may stay there for months or even a year. In either case, track them and discuss their status at these meetings so that no potential client falls through the crack. There may be many clients you will ultimately convert that have been in your Zone of Client Opportunity for more than a year and you won't even know it. Reviewing this information on a regular basis reminds you that they are out there. Without these meetings, you will potentially lose track of many of these outliers over time. However you do it, put a process in place that allows you to know what happens to every single client that contacts you or that enters your Zone of Client Opportunity or both.

In later chapters, we will cover in more detail the conversion process within the Zone of Client Opportunity as well as the process for growing your business in a profitable way because both are ultimately critical to your success.

CHAPTER SUMMARY POINTS:

- A framework is a structured way to apply strategic objectives to help you execute both short and long-term strategies. Building your business around this framework will ultimately help you create an executable strategy for long-term success.

- In an elective aesthetic cosmetic practice, the framework consists of four major sections: The Market, Your Brand in the Market, The Zone of Client Opportunity, and the Zone of the Continuously Growing and Profitable Business. In addition to this framework, you must have a plan to address all four areas in order to be successful.

- While all components of the framework interact with each other, the one area that potentially has the greatest impact is conversion within the Zone of Client Opportunity. If you are successful in moving potential clients from the market into your business structure (the Zone of Client Opportunity), you have accomplished a significant step in the process to becoming a highly profitable business. But if you can't convert, you have effectively wasted time and money spent to move them to that point.

SECTION 4

YOUR BRAND

Chapter 9

ESTABLISHING YOUR IDENTITY (BRANDING)

*"If your work is becoming uninteresting, so are you. Work is an
inanimate thing and can be made lively and interesting only
by injecting yourself into it. Your job is only as big as you are."*

George C. Hubbs

I n the early 1970's, Phil Knight brought a small company from
Eugene, Oregon into the athletic footwear marketplace by selling
track shoes from the back of his wood-paneled station wagon. From
these humble beginnings, this small company has since unleashed a
wave of change worldwide. Through incredibly effective branding and
marketing efforts, its patented "Just Do It" mantra and signature logo
have literally become an iconic force worldwide. In so doing, Nike
effectively established itself as a household brand name and secured its
place in history. Nike became the de facto standard for running shoes.
An entire industry changed because you were not considered an elite
runner unless you had Nike's on. All other shoe companies benefited
from Nike's marketing but Nike always got the premium business they
wanted despite the fact that their biggest competitor, Adidas, had been in
business far longer. What should this teach you? That marching into the
aesthetic marketplace, providers of elective aesthetics must do the same
thing: establish a rock-solid brand, though arguably on a smaller and
probably more local, level.

The act of branding is an unsung, often overlooked force in business. Without it, your business becomes simply another name in the phone book. With it, your business becomes a recognizable entity capable of withstanding changing market forces. Branding is easily the most important element you must consider when designing your business.

Quite simply put, it tells your client base who you are, what you are, and how you differ from the competition. It makes sense that everything said about, seen, and identified with your company should promote a unifying message which will then further your brand identity.

According to Wikipedia, Pears Soap was the first registered commercial brand. Since then, literally thousands of brands have been introduced into the public space—some more effectively than others. A successful brand gets that way through a series of coordinated and carefully calculated strategies aimed at creating a relationship with the consumer that extends to multiple levels. To accomplish this, a brand needs to have a look and feel compatible with the industry it represents and it must be carefully constructed to attract attention from a very specific target audience. As such, the end consumer must be identified and described prior to construct of a brand identity. Effective branding, simply put, is communicating to the right clientele through the proper media at the right time over time.

The first rule of business is, don't open your doors without first establishing a good brand strategy. But branding takes time. You don't just walk in the first day you are open and tell the world you are the highest quality provider of a product or service and everyone just agrees to pay you a higher rate than your competition. Develop a strategy and stay with it. Be patient, be persistent, and get feedback on how your brand strategy is working from your clients. And react accordingly. This is top priority for the long-term health of your business. Know what you are and who you are and the rest will follow.

The next rule is Applied Marketing. Marketing is the process of planning and executing a concept—pricing, promotion and distribution. As such, marketing is effectively a means by which to disseminate your brand to a target consumer in a calculated and strategic manner. To accomplish this, you've already identified your target consumer; the next goal is to identify how best to reach this individual. A carefully executed marketing plan must be designed to educate on the attributes of your brand, your product and service offerings and your ability to execute on your commitments to clients. You must do so in a language common, identifiable, and comfortable to this specific consumer. Your message must be consistent, reinforce your brand at all times, and must resonate across multiple media.

Although the brand itself may be slightly modified at times, at its core it must always be identifiable with a consistent message. For example, your brand name should be reflected in your website domain name, your yellow page ad, your signage, your business cards, and in all other collateral media disseminated to your target audience. Any significant wavering from this core message will be seen as confusing to your audience and have the potential to erode your brand identity. Keep your message simple, to the point, and above all, keep it consistent. In simplest terms, effective marketing is the process of shouting it from the rooftops but only having your target audience hear. Without effective marketing, your practice may be good but no one will know that. So how do we do this?

One of the hardest lessons I learned after residency was how to market. As residents, while we are taught how to save lives, we are never taught how to how to manage, grow and build our own business. From the day I left residency, I was inundated with various ways in which to market my practice—some good and some not so good. The immediate problem I had was not only had I not been educated in marketing principles in medical school, I was also never taught how to even evaluate marketing options. Add in the changes brought about by the meteoric growth and adoption of the internet and you have a recipe for spending a whole lot of money without getting the right kind of results. You do not want to do marketing promotion by trial and error anymore then you have to. In a later chapter, you will see reference to split testing and trials as controlled and valuable ways to determine how to get attention from potential clients. As compared to advertising on a venue such as a billboard, these approaches are far less expensive and easier to track.

Although there are regional variations in marketing, there are also some tried and true marketing options that span all regions. Let's start with breaking marketing down into two types—Internal and External—and then we can subdivide them further. Internal marketing involves using your staff and client base as marketing sources. In a later chapter, we will discuss a full range of marketing strategies based purely on referrals from staff, clients, partners, and others.

External marketing, on the other hand, is what we think of in more traditional terms and may include actions such as traditional advertising, event-based marketing, and even free advertising. Because there are so many different ways to advertise today and so many different results that you can ultimately achieve, you must really examine this possibility very carefully before implementing it. One of the simplest examples of external marketing is the billboard. For many of you it probably strikes you as crazy that someone might still use billboard advertising as part of their strategy but in many cases this approach actually works very well. But location is critical as well as the understanding that one billboard is probably not enough. Marketing statistics support the concept that three billboards containing the same information within a 15 mile linear drive will get you ten times the results. If a billboard campaign costs you $10,000 and delivers you three new clients with an average profit per client at $2,500 then it isn't worth it. The best way to approach traditional advertising is to work with a local marketing consultant who can show you delivered return on investment through referrals and who has some basic knowledge of your business. Whether you are utilizing print media, billboard, local TV or radio spots, or any other type of advertising, we recommend that you pay a local marketing consultant on performance as compared to a salary or fixed fee basis. If you can't track results of a specific program or you cannot actually speak to someone else who has run the program, then don't do it. Marketing costs money and you need to spend money to make money; but the money you spend on marketing should be tied directly back to a result deposited in your bank account.

Event based marketing is a different subject. This type of marketing occurs when you do an open house or a seminar. Don't look at an open house, and we mean not just the one you do at your grand opening but one you probably should do annually, as a cheap way to reward existing clientele or draw in a few new interested parties. An open house in the elective aesthetic business can draw in potential clients who are reluctant to come in for a one-on-one consultation but who are much more comfortable having their questions answered in a group setting. One of the biggest problems we face in any type of business is the act of developing trust with a potential client. The biggest barrier to this initially is that the potentially client simply doesn't know you. And while your accolades and website picture might comfort them somewhat, an open house allows them to come in, shake your hand, and actually meet you face to face. To be outstanding in this business you must be great at capturing the business that comes to you for a consultation. But you have to get them in first before you can convert them.

Throwing an effective event like an open house or an educational seminar doesn't happen just by sending an email out or simply posting a sign on your front. You need to be more proactive. Send a mailer to your clients and targeted potential clients; reward your clients for bringing people to your open house; put together an email blast; talk to your strategic partners (such as dentists, dermatologists, oculoplastic surgeons, etc.) and have them advertise your open house. Take this event very seriously because while you may spend thousands on the event, you may easily double that in profit with just two new clients. Hold the open house as an educational seminar for introduction of a new facial injectable and ask the manufacturer to help sponsor the event. Your best marketing strategy will always be to get potential clients in your door. Let me say that again: your best marketing strategy will be to get potential clients in your door. Traditional means of securing new patients through email contact, phone contact, or contacts through your advertising efforts may never be as effective as simply getting them to come meet you personally at one of these events.

Promotion is a big part of getting your name out there. What you promote must be strategically designed to assist in the development of your brand identity but also aimed at getting out your specific message. Be creative and speak to your specific client and they will ultimately break down your doors to see you!

CHAPTER SUMMARY POINTS:

- Branding is the message; applied marketing and advertising are the means for spreading this message.

- Develop a core message, continuously reinforce it, and never waver from the central theme.

- There are many ways to market. Know which specific methods work best for you and your local market.

SECTION 5

YOUR MARKET

Chapter 10

DEFINING YOUR MARKET (FOCUSING)

*"The whole world steps aside for the man
who knows where he is going."*

Author Unknown

So who do we create our brand for? The first step in both starting as well as building your practice is identification of the target client. Fishermen understand that to catch a particular type of fish, they must use a specific lure or fly or net, in a specific location, at a particular time. Different lures, flies, or nets capture specific fish. You don't catch a trout with a net, but you do attract a river trout's attention with certain flies used at certain times of the year and in specific parts of the country. As an example, 85 fly patterns have been proven to be effective year-round in the upper Midwest.

In establishing a client base, think along similar lines. To communicate with your target audience, you must first know who they are. You must know their age, their race, their income level and their educational level. These factors are all critical in communicating to your target audience and will help identify the location of these clients, and how they like to be spoken to and what will attract their interest. In essence, by isolating and identifying these individual preferences, we can better familiarize ourselves with our clients and create trust.

So now that you know who your target client is, identify their specific goals. What are they looking to improve, how much downtime are they willing to accept, how fast are they looking for results, how long do they want these results to last, and how much are they willing to spend? Every one of these questions is critical to know before you meet this client. And, when you do, you must confirm that your assumptions are in line with theirs. If not, unrealistic expectations, either to low or to high, are created and your brand becomes far less effective. In the words of the famous advertising copywriter and ad agency founder David Ogilvy, a brand is... "The intangible sum of a product's attributes: its name, packaging, and price, its history, its reputation and the way it's advertised." By virtue of the definition given by Ogilvy any of the attributes listed (packaging, price, and reputation) can be adversely affected by poor branding. You do not want to give away your profit simply because you ineffectively branded your practice nor do you want your reputation to be less than it really is.

CHAPTER SUMMARY POINTS:

- To effectively market to your client, you must first know everything about this potential client. And to understand this, you must know your market.

- Once you know this client, you must then try and understand their specific goals.

- And once you know their goals, be clear in your initial discussions and make sure to set realistic expectations.

Chapter 11

BUILDING CLIENT OPPORTUNITY: THE FOUR P'S OF MARKETING & ADVERTISING

"There are no secrets to success. It is the result of preparation, hard work, and learning from failure."

Colin Powell

It has been said that "marketing is an art not a science". But with computer technology and the rise of the internet this statement needs to be revised to read: "Marketing is an art that should be based on science". Using demographics, we can track purchasing decisions to the degree that we can isolate and segment any group we want. And we can perform split testing to see which words in our ads make the most sense in attracting the kind of client we actually want. We can segment the market and isolate certain customer types very effectively because people rarely use newspapers or billboards any more to make decisions; they use computers and other people's opinions. You may think that the four P's of marketing, product, place, promotion, and price don't apply anymore because of this new technology but they do now and always will. What has changed is how we execute our strategy regarding these 4 P's. And to be effective, you must have a strategy addressing all four.

Marketing is one of those costs, that is often hard to find calculate true value from. If I know what the four P's are, is that enough to make me successful? Not usually. In today's world you cannot afford to spend money on anything that doesn't lead to a return on investment, and marketing is no exception. You must be able to track your marketing programs and continually assess their performance. Sometimes it is as easy as asking your customers who come in how they made the decision to come to you. But while that approach can be relatively effective, it doesn't always tell you if you ran your marketing campaign in the most cost effective manner possible. Most people are satisfied with breakeven or better campaigns but to me a break-even approach is never acceptable. To pass my test, a campaign must demonstrate relevant return on investment, it must not compromise your business reputation or goals, and it should ultimately position you for even better returns on future campaigns. Keep in mind that high quality marketing is a cumulative but generally a not linear function.

Let's look at return on investment using the following example. If you invested $10,000 in the stock market and received a one-time pay off in a 12 month period of $2,000, then you would have received a 20% return on your investment. Very nice return in my book. But what if instead you could have realized a 40% return on investment? That would be a much better scenario. If you had the option of spending $10,000 on marketing and your choice was between paying for billboards that could potentially attract three new clients or an internet pay per click campaign that also returned three new clients, how would you know which was a better decision? If you spent $10,000 on an internet-based pay per click advertising campaign designed to drive traffic to your website but you got three initial new clients the question is what else did you get? If the pay per click advertising drove enough extra traffic to your website that it effectively increased your search engine rankings resulting in another 2-4 clients three months down the road, with this scenario, you would have achieved a 100% return on your investment. This is a much better solution. So how do you know which way to go? To analyze this, you must understand the four P's of marketing and you must know, or pay a consultant who does, to execute a marketing plan based on what is best for your specific business. The internet is not always the best solution; sometimes billboards are. And sometimes the best marketing approach changes from one month to the next.

The first of these, product choice, is critical. Without proper product choice, you can spend large amounts of money promoting products that don't fit your core capabilities, products that don't allow you to be competitive or profitable, or products that simply do not fit within your core competency. While all of us would choose to offer a full complement of products and services to every patient that walks into the office, this approach is not always practical. Defining what lies at the core of your practice is one of the most important early decisions you can make. Are you a body only doctor or are you a facial specialist? Are you a dermatologist or an internist, family practitioner, or OB-GYN interested in augmenting practice revenue by adding elective products and services? In following chapters, we will review product choices and discuss why you should or should not incorporate them into your practice.

As noted earlier in this book, the aesthetic industry is a broad discipline and encompasses a wide array of procedures. And while over time most core procedures remain the same, subtle variations are continually being offered making the industry confusing not only to the consumer but also to the practitioner. From this array of choices, your first responsibility is designing a menu of products and services. Next, each of these offerings must have some level of marketing associated with them---even if it consists of nothing more than cross selling facial filler injections to your BOTOX Cosmetic clients, or medical skincare to clients undergoing breast augmentation. But choosing which products to offer can be as difficult as figuring out how best to promote them.

Choosing specific products to offer requires that you analyze your capabilities as well as the market's ability to support that product. A good example is the facial injectable. To effectively enter this marketplace, you need an appropriate infrastructure in place to support these clients—before, during, and after their procedure. This requires knowledge of available facial injectables as well as an experienced injector. Whether you, the physician, or a physician-extender actually performs the injections, appropriate training should be undertaken before actually offering this service. Injectable training should focus on properties of the various injectables, applicable facial anatomy, aftercare, and treatment of adverse events.

While some physicians perform all procedures themselves, others prefer to delegate them to an appropriately trained extender. If you choose the latter option and don't initially have the resources to hire a full-time nurse injector, one option is to hire this person on a percentage basis of gross injection revenue. And while this may be helpful in some instances, keep in mind that the major downfall is that with delegation, you lose a certain degree of control as well as scheduling flexibility over this area of your practice.

As we keep emphasizing, product selection is a critical element in operating a very high performing practice. You must assure that the market will support your entry into it, you must have the resources to support a high quality patient friendly service, and you must have the patients and discipline to launch the product the right way. If you choose the wrong product, you will not only reduce or eliminate your profitability for that product but you may also be forced to reduce resources you have available to promote other products that are better positioned. In addition, by introducing the wrong product, you may hurt your reputation causing a downturn in other areas of your practice as a result of disgruntled patients. The end result is that your ability to cultivate high quality referrals from clients either diminishes or goes away entirely. Product selection must be done via a structured process for you to be successful.

In a later chapter, we will return to this theme and provide you with a checklist as well as information on market research and product launch criteria to help you position yourself properly. If you have existing products that are under-performing, you can also use this information to reposition these products to achieve the market share and profitability you deserve.

CHAPTER SUMMARY POINTS:

- The 4 P's of marketing are critical to success and include the following:
    - Product
    - Place
    - Promotion
    - Price

Chapter 12

PRODUCT – WHAT ARE YOU SELLING AND WHY?

"We owe a lot to Thomas Edison - if it wasn't for him, we'd be watching television by candlelight."

Milton Berle

If the notion of the four P's sounds complicated, it really isn't. Let's start by focusing on the first P – product. Products in our cosmetic practice include the various kinds of surgery we might perform, the non-invasive products that we either create or have the right to sell such as skincare lines, invasive products such as injectables or Botulinum toxin type A products, services done with things like Lasers or other types of capital medical. They are all products and all can be sold by most medical professionals with the appropriate training and resources. For some the decision is to just sell everything they can sell because it gives them a better chance of driving revenue to their practices. This strategy backfires for most that choose to start this way. There are a number of businesses in this country who do sell virtually all available cosmetic healthcare products effectively but they are all experienced practices who didn't start that way. They built their practices and added products as they went along.

The decision on what products to sell depends on a number of factors. Start up cost is usually the first thing to consider. If you want to sell a procedure that dramatically reduces acne, for example, you will need to determine if you can afford to start that business. If you have to inventory the drug needed and buy or lease the laser to activate the drug it may be too expensive to get into. In many cases adding a product line will depend on how quickly you can get new patients to cover your initial start up costs. If you have a strong base of existing clients who would want the service then you can defer your start up costs very quickly and make it possible to get into the business. However, if you are cash and credit-poor, and can't buy the technology and inventory you need, you may have to wait. Start-up costs are a reality in any product line you decide to add. If the product line is necessary to develop your practice the right way there are always ways to get it started credit or not. Contact us directly if you are in that situation for assistance via our contact info provided at the back of this book.

Let's say for purposes of this discussion that you do have the start up costs of a new product line covered. Now you need to decide whether or not to actually get into the business. The very first question you need to answer is going to be; "Is there actually a market for this product that I can address?" This question has two halves that must both be addressed. The first half of the statement; "is there a market" depends on demographics such as age, available income, growth or decline of population, and other factors. If you are trying to roll out your new acne elimination product and you are in a market in which the total population of 13 – 25 year olds is less than 1000 people you probably don't have a market. The second half of that statement is also critical because there may be a market for your new acne elimination product but if you are up against competitors who have been in that market for years ahead of you and you don't have a strong client base to self refer from then you may be looking at a losing proposition also. When we discuss promotion in chapter 9 you will better understand that promotion cannot overcome all deficiencies in your ability to profitably market a product not matter how much money you throw at it.

There are plenty of vendors in the world who are interested in having you carry their product or service. Vendors, who sell products like acne elimination, will have demographics and market data to support why you should enter a particular product line market. In many cases they refer to their marketing collateral as "Cost Justification" documents or marketing documents. In reality most of these pre made marketing documents are really "justifying cost" so that you will make a commitment to buy their products. Vendors are valuable to your practice and you should listen to what they have to say and take their information as an important data point in your decision process but don't base your whole decision on that information alone. Do the research yourself. Ask the vendor to give you references on customers who have actually seen the results they advertise and call those references to verify. Also ask the vendor to give you the names of some of their clients who haven't realized the return on investment they advertise so you can find out why. They won't want to do this but push the issue until you get an answer. Telling the vendor that you know that results vary based on what actions the customer actually takes in introducing and promoting their product so they should be comfortable in letting you talk to their customers who haven't been successful so you can find out what not to do also. Any vendor who won't give you this probably needs to be ruled out of your product decision process.

Beyond evaluating whether there is a market and whether you can service it you must also take a very serious look at your competition for that product line. How are they positioning themselves with the messages they send to the potential client population? If they are a low price provider in a lower middle class market and that market is the center or your practice then you have to determine if you can get enough volume to be in that market. Your other option is to try and displace them and take a leading share position away from them. Do they have enough brand equity that you can't displace them but you could take a slice of the market and still be profitable? You will have to do a return on investment review as indicated earlier to make this decision.

Once you launch a product you will see that competitor react in many cases and you need to be prepared in advance with a follow up strategy. Will you lower your price, run special volume based promotions, raise your price and offer a premium level service, or do nothing and wait for the market to normalize. If you have a strong committed client base you may not have to worry about this at all but if you choose to ignore the competition then you may be missing an opportunity to add to your client base through a new product line. Paying attention and having some flexibility when dealing with competition is the most important thing you can do with your new product line or when you want to advance the profitability of an established one. There are published statistics that show that the first person to market with a product or service gets 50% of the market for the first 5 years. Either be first or make sure you are a fast enough follower to get the lion's share of the other 50%.

Markets grow, remain steady, or decline. Very few business consultants would tell you to enter a market that is not growing. Fortunately, other than some unusual market areas affected by declining population or more rapid aging of the population, the cosmetic healthcare industry is growing at a very healthy rate. This is due primarily to the advancing age of the baby boomers and media hype about how good you can look at every age. We have the technology today to make the media look very smart and every physician practice that has the desire can get into the business and take a profitable piece. There are a number of tools available to help you understand your specific market dynamics with regards to the growth of the market and the dynamics at play in getting more share of that market.

All products in the cosmetic healthcare market have a target audience you want will want to focus on. The target audience doesn't consist of all the people who buy a particular product. It is more important to think of your target as the core group of clients you will need to build your practice around. It should be a mix of clients that represent those that never leave you because they always want something done, those that come and go as they age and want additional services in blocks, and those that come to you once and never comeback because they fixed the one thing they had a concern about. This mix will have a lot to do with determining which products can be sold profitably or not. If you have a large number of customers who never leave you and you want to add BOTOX Cosmetic to your product lines offered, it probably makes sense since BOTOX Cosmetic is a maintenance product that gets used over and over again. If you have a lot of one timers who leave happy and don't return then a product like BOTOX Cosmetic wouldn't make sense. In chapter 8 we will go into much greater detail on finding out which products can be sold profitably by your practice in the particular markets you want to do business in.

There are very lucrative markets in most cities in the United States for Cosmetic Healthcare Products and Services. If you plan properly, understand the market dynamics, determine who you will be competing with and how they will affect your position, and if you have the necessary start up costs you can go boldly into most of the product markets. One of the biggest mistakes we see is when someone successfully launches a product line they then think they do not have to do all the same research and analysis when it comes time to launch the next product line. You should get more efficient at the process but one successful launch is just one successful launch. Be disciplined and you will get the best results each time you launch a product line and with that will come greater cash flow and profitability.

CHAPTER SUMMARY POINTS:

- More important than what you sell is why you actually sell it.

- To determine what to sell, consider:
    - Start-up costs
    - Demand
    - Choice of vendors
    - Competition

Chapter 13

PLACE – WHAT MARKET AREA DO YOU WANT TO SELL IN?

"Whether you think you can or think you can't – you are right."

Henry Ford

Evaluating the market takes some time and energy but as you begin your practice it is well worth the effort. Not only will it help you understand where to establish your physical location but should also give you insight into the specific products and services you should sell. You cannot use a "Field of Dreams" strategy, build a place of business and hope customers will come, and expect to create the success you want. While you could get lucky and build a practice without any research and open it to great success, I wouldn't advocate that approach. The real question is how do you do meaningful market research at a cost that makes sense.

The first thing you should do is call the local chamber of commerce and obtain their annual report for the market service area you wish to be a part of. For the most part, this report will be free but in some cases it may cost as little as $25. The most important thing about a chamber report is that it is going to give you a demographic based view of the market. And one of the things demographics will show you is income and population distribution. If you are looking for medium to higher income areas ($75,000 per year and up), then you need to identify that specific area to locate your business in.

There are two other important criteria to consider other than just income. Baby boomers and their parents are the richest generations in history and they are the primary buyers of aesthetic services. A local Chamber of Commerce report will also show you an age distribution of the population. This level of granularity is important because in most major cities you will find more than one income distribution area in which you could locate and you don't want to make the mistake of ending up in the wrong one. The biggest buying group for aesthetic services is between the ages of 32 and 72. If you take income distribution statistics and overlay them with age-related statistics you end up with a market sweet spot for aesthetic services at persons who make more than $75,000 and who are older than 32 but younger than 72. Take that a step further and make sure you isolate a market with at least 100,000 people in it that meet your targets on income and age so that you will have a stream of business to sustain your business targets.

Another important factor in choosing your market and location is the amount of established competition. Entering a saturated market will obviously make finding enough clients will be difficult to near impossible. While a market doesn't have to be free from competition there should not be more than 5 practices per 100,000 people if you don't already have an established position yourself in that market. There are exceptions to this. One is if you have an established base of non-aesthetic services (such as in a family practice or dermatology entity). In this situation, you already have a client base for referrals and that alone can be enough to add aesthetic services to your mix. The other factor is if you are in a market that has unusually high incomes. An example of this would be Beverly Hills California or Boca Raton Florida. In those markets, expect to see somewhat different criteria in terms of population size and competition. Instead of a typical rate of 80 aesthetic services per 1000 people per year, their rate might be as high as 150 per 1000 people because of the geographic location and local environment. Always evaluate the degree of competition in any market you choose to do business in.

Even if you are already established, you still need to know local competition for a service or product line you would like to offer. You invest a lot of time and money in technology and people to provide these services, so know what you are up against so that you can position yourself well initially and have a strategy to dominate the market in the long run.

To market one product or several products, you still must follow the same process to decide how and when to go to market. The following steps are necessary:

- Define what the market is via chamber of commerce data and MSA data

- Make sure age and income distribution are capable of meeting the requirements for number of patients and number of revenue.

- If they don't, you don't want to be in this business. Criteria include the following:

- 100,000 or more people 32 – 72

- Income of $75,000 or greater. For people over 65, the report should show an income estimate based on their taxes.

Analyze competition and have no more than 5 other practices offering the same service per 100,000 people within that age and income bracket. If the potential market meets all these criteria, then you have a very good chance of building a profitable aesthetic service within it. Further analyze potential profitability based on data we will give you in subsequent chapters, but understand that for most practices the most critical variable is really your ability to deliver the service then the actual market itself.

CHAPTER SUMMARY POINTS:

- Knowing your market will help you to determine where to establish your practice as well as what products and services to actually offer potential clients.

- To evaluate your market, consider the following variables:

    - Average age of the population
    - Average income distribution
    - Amount of established competition
    - Products & services currently being offered

Chapter 14

PROMOTION – HOW WILL PEOPLE KNOW WHAT YOU ARE SELLING?

"There are some people who live in a dream world,
and there are some who face reality; and then
there are those who turn one into the other."

Douglas Everett

S o who do we promote to? The first step in both starting as well as building your practice is identification of your target client. Fishermen understand that to catch a particular type of fish, they must use a specific lure or fly or net, in a specific location, at a particular time. Different lures, flies, or nets capture specific fish. You don't catch a trout with a net, but you do attract a river trout's attention with flies. And flies used at certain times of year and in specific parts of the country vary.

This gets back to first identifying and then directly speaking to your target audience. If your client is 25-35 years old and interested in Breast Augmentation and located in the San Diego marketplace, their look, feel, and language of your message should speak to this. In contrast, if you are appealing to a more mature 45-65 year old New England base of clientele, your message must resonate with them but most likely in a much different manner.

In establishing a client base, you must think along similar lines. To communicate with your target audience, you must know who they are.

Identify their age, their race, their income level and their educational level. These factors are all critical in communicating to a target audience and help identify location of these clients, their particular spending habits, and how they like to be spoken to and with. In essence, by isolating and identifying these specific variables, we can better familiarize ourselves with our clients and create trust.

The first step involves analyzing logistics of your local target population. Depending upon where you plan to practice, people spend money differently. While breast augmentation may be cocktail party chatter in Los Angeles, it certainly is not in smaller towns. If people are not talking about cosmetic surgery, your marketing should reflect this and suggest a more private, confidential feel to your practice environment. And while you may get away with more brash, cutting-edge graphics (and even a billboard) in Miami, you probably will not in small town Nebraska. Again, speak to your target audience specifically and pointedly and remember that they need to identify with you before they trust you with their appearance.

Another variable to assess is the willingness to spend money on cosmetic procedures. With all due respect to Cleveland, when I lived there I noticed a lower level of interest in cosmetic enhancement as compared to other major metropolitan areas such as Los Angeles and Miami. Know what you are getting into before you get into it. Otherwise, you will be setting yourself up for not only extreme disappointment but, more importantly, some very lean financial years.

So now that you know who your target client is, identify their specific goals. What is it that they are looking to improve, how much downtime are they willing to accept, how fast are they looking for results, how long do they want these results to last, and how much are they willing to spend? Every one of these questions must be answered before you meet this client. And, when you do, confirm that your assumptions are in line with theirs. If not, unrealistic expectations are created and your brand becomes an ineffective logo. In the words of the famous advertising copywriter and ad agency founder David Ogilvy, a brand is…"The intangible sum of a product's attributes: its name, packaging, and price, its history, its reputation and the way it's advertised."

As previously discussed, the first order of business is not opening your doors without first establishing a good brand. Know what you are and who you are and the rest will follow. Start by knowing the rules. The first rule is that your branding must be deliberate and it must be consistent. The next rule is to utilize Applied Marketing. Marketing is the process of planning and executing a concept—pricing, promotion and distribution. As such, marketing is effectively a means by which to disseminate your brand to a target consumer in a calculated and strategic manner. To accomplish this, you've already identified your target consumer; the next goal is to identify how best to reach this individual. A carefully executed marketing plan must be designed to educate this consumer on the attributes of your brand and do so in a language common, identifiable, and comfortable to this specific consumer. Your message must be consistent, reinforce your brand at all times, and must resonate across multiple media. Although the brand itself may be slightly modified at times, at its core it must always be identifiable with a consistent message. For example, your brand name should be reflected in your website domain name, your yellow page ad, your signage, your business cards, and in all other collateral media disseminated to your target audience. Any significant wavering from this core message may be seen as confusing to your audience and have the potential to erode brand identity. Keep your message simple and to the point. And above all, keep it consistent.

In the most basic terms, effective marketing is the process of shouting it from the rooftops but only having your target audience hear. Without effective marketing, your practice may be good but no one will know. So how do we do this?

Marketing can effectively be broken into two types--External and Internal—and then subdivided further. Internet marketing is currently recognized as one of the most effectiveness venues for external marketing. The first step in marketing to the internet user is through creation of a practice website. This site should utilize a domain name that reflects your specific brand but which is easily located and chosen for effective search engine optimization. And the site should be attractive and easy to browse.

In addition, it should not only educate but also draw your consumer in. In techie terms, such a site is referred to as garnering "eyeballs" (people come to the site) and "sticky" (people stay at the site). These two criteria are essential to the effectiveness of your web presence. The longer that a browser stays at and is engaged by your site, the more likely that he or she will be converted to use your services. To accomplish this, speak to your target consumer using language, diction, colors, and pictures that this person will identify with. Your site should selectively speak to your consumer and strengthen your brand presence.

But what good is an attractive website if your consumers cannot find you in the first place? I call this the "Picasso in the basement" phenomenon. A good website should be optimized for search terms specific to your industry. This enables search engines to actually find you, list you, and direct appropriate clientele to your site. Once you have been listed, or "indexed" by the search engines, the next step is to climb the proverbial ladder. You can choose to either be listed under the pay per click category or through the process of organic optimization. While there is really no perfect scenario, they each have their own respective advantages and disadvantages.

Pay per click, or PPC marketing, refers to the process whereby you actually bid for clicks. In essence, you pay a certain amount each time someone clicks on your web link. The higher you are willing to pay each time, the higher you are ranked. Once you reach your budgeted cap, your link drops off and the person below you takes your space. PPC marketing has the advantage of quickly securing ranking although it can be a much pricier way to secure top ranking in the long run.

Organic optimization is a complex phenomenon where search engines effectively determine your relevance to the search term entered and then list a series of sites accordingly. This process is too complex to describe here in depth and the rules unfortunately seem to change on a regular basis. Suffice to say that the search engines intents are to identify sites that have keyword appropriate content and then rank them based on relevance. A basic way to ensure that your site is relevant is to always keep your material fresh and update copy on a regular basis. This doesn't necessarily mean that you need to rewrite your website every week. Many people freshen optimization by adding a BLOG (or Weblog) to their site. Articles can then be added on a routine basis so that Google, Yahoo, and other search engines identify this new content and raise their relevance levels accordingly.

My personal recommendation is to invest in a good SEO (search engine optimization) and website hosting company. In the long run, this type of marketing tends to have far greater ROI (return on investment) than other costly outreaches such as radio, television, and print ads and can be a highly successful means of reaching your target audience.

CHAPTER SUMMARY POINTS:

- Nets work great for fish but not for clients. Know the type of client you are looking for before you look for them and your search will be much easier.

- Knowing your target audience enables you to properly speak to your target audience.

- Know the following about your target audience:
    - Their age
    - Their race
    - Their income level
    - Their level of education
    - Their spending habits
    - How they like to be spoken to

- Avoid the "Picasso in the basement" phenomenon

- Design a good website and make sure that it is effectively optimized

Chapter 15

PRICE – DISCIPLINE AND COMPETITIVENESS

"There is no elevator to success. You have to take the stairs."

Author Unknown

How important is price? It depends on the scope of the product line you are trying to sell, the marketplace you are trying to sell it in, your capital position, and your tolerance to vary profit targets to win more business. Price elasticity is the study of how consumers react to price. Some markets have no elasticity at all which means that consumer decisions are not based on pricing at all. These types of markets have very distinctly different products or services offered by very few providers. In the aesthetic market place price elasticity appears to be moderate. Consumers will go somewhere other than their existing provider if price varies enough. If you are providing BOTOX Cosmetic; it doesn't mean you need to charge the lowest price per unit because consumers do see value in the abilities of their injector.

How much higher can you set your price? It depends on the quality of the relationship you have established with your clients. Clients who see value in the relationship with you along with the products and services you provide are far less elastic on price. You can't charge them whatever you want but, in most cases, you can predictably set a 20% premium over the lowest local market price. You will need to experiment to see how your clients and the market value your service. If someone is spending $500 on BOTOX

Cosmetic injections will they stay with you if you are at $525 for the same amount of BOTOX Cosmetic? They will if you have demonstrated value in your services and have established a solid relationship with that client.

In any market, if you price yourself too low you risk strapping yourself with lower profits and may permanently establish a reputation as being the low cost provider. For some, this is okay but we don't recommend this strategy. It is very difficult, if not impossible, to raise your rates beyond some reasonable inflationary amount, once customers have become used to low prices. Price your products and services too high and you may not get enough business to cover fixed costs. You may also be seen as arrogant and potential customers may think you are out of touch with the needs of the mainstream customer.

Given price sensitivity, how do you make sure you set pricing correctly so that you don't create the problems listed above? Start by doing market research on pricing before offering any service or product. Whether you are opening a new practice or simply adding a product line, this step is important. Have your staff make phone calls to other local providers. We recommend having one of your female staff members make these calls because the places we have called feel that women overall come across as more legitimate. If that proves to be the case, you will potentially retrieve better information overall. Perform frequent internet searches to locate and evaluate competitor's websites and identify pricing levels or temporary incentives. Use online and paper based yellow pages to also find information regarding your competition. Assign a specific staff member as the pricing researcher for your market. And streamlines the process by establishing a process that guides them through where, how and when to check pricing status.

Pricing is not a one-time event. Review pricing on a regular basis to see that you aren't pricing yourself out of the local market as well as making sure you are not too low either. There will always be a point where your capacity to service new clients is limited because you would have to hire new staff to do so. At that point, the last thing you want to do is to have pricing that is too low. In that situation, you have a full schedule and you want to make sure you are maximizing your hourly profit by setting the right pricing.

If you have capacity to fill and you just can't fill it your tendency will be to lower price to drive in new clients but you must do so very carefully. Lowering price point in a market where information is so easy to come by means that your existing clients will also find out and want this same discount. In some cases, that is okay because your total profit per hour is based on the total profit you make in a day divided by the number of hours you staff your business. If you have empty hours, your profit per hour will be less. The simplest example would be to say that if you have 10% of your total capacity available and unfilled and you can lower price by 5% to fill that time, it is probably a good idea. But be careful not to fluctuate your pricing too frequently or appear to always be having a sale.

As part of your pricing research process, check specials that could potentially steal profitable pieces of your business. We have found the best way to execute this is to have a quarterly pricing review with your team. Have staff members participate by asking them to sign up for competitor's mailing lists. These lists will typically be distributed via email/newsletters. In addition to collecting information via mail or online sources, also assign staff to review trade journals and local publications for ads focused on pricing or specials. Conduct quarterly meetings to renew this data and determine if you need to raise your price, lower your price, keep the same pricing structure, or offer temporary incentives. Pricing reviews are especially important 60 days prior to a holiday (such as Mother's Day or Valentine's Day) because so many providers offer promotions during these periods.

In the cosmetic healthcare market, pricing tends to be similar from one provider to another. The key is to secure the patient the first time they are looking for something and then keep them for the remainder of their needs. For example, if you perform their liposuction and they are happy with their results, they shouldn't need to shop for BOTOX Cosmetic injections when they can just get them from you. But keep in mind that some customers are so price conscious that they will shop for every little thing they want. We recommend that when you do an initial consultation that you offer package pricing so that you can lock them into a service for as many of their needs as possible up front. By implementing combination treatments or package pricing, you effectively lock the patient in for a longer treatment period and, for the most part, probably offer them a more comprehensive and optimal result in the long run.

One you have established baseline pricing and have set up a process to monitor price in your market, you must have a strategy for addressing pricing opportunities that will arise. Understanding your average profit per client is critical. The simplest way to accomplish this is by taking your total revenue in any given category--let's use skin resurfacing for our example--and subtracting all direct costs, any specific variable costs used for that procedure or product type, and then subtracting indirect costs (overhead) such as a portion of your receptionist and rent. The portion of your overhead that gets subtracted should be directly proportionate to the amount of revenue the service provides relative to your overall revenue. Let's walk through an example for skin resurfacing:

Nurse working hours	**40**
Hourly rate	**$40.00**
Benefits @26%	**$10.40**
Total Costs	**$2,016.00**
Botox Cost/Unit	**$6.00**
Botox used for 10 patients	**$250.00**
Total Botox Cost for 10 patients	**$1,500.00**
Total overall costs	**$3,516.00**
Cost per patient	**$351.60**
Revenue	
10 patients at $12/unit	**$300.00**
Net loss per patient	**-$51.60**

Table 15.1

Knowing that you have a $325 profit margin per client for this specific procedure provides you with substantially more information to make decisions about whether to run a promotion. In the example, above you are spreading your fixed costs of $40,000 over a total of 840 procedures for a fixed cost per procedure of $47. If you have capacity, (meaning you have staff available to do more work and your machine is available) then you have the ability to add procedures without adding additional fixed costs which will ultimately allow you to lower your cost per procedure. If through a promotion you add 100 procedures to the total through a promotion you now have 940 procedures or a new fixed cost per procedure of $42. That drops overall cost by $5 per procedure or $4,700 ($5x940). In this example you could spend as much as $47 per procedure to get those additional 100 procedures and still break even. With that said, your best bet would be to offer a $25 incentive towards skin resurfacing to attract more business.

With two important exceptions, all pricing decisions should be made based on either profitably filling or being able to gain enough volume at a high enough price to make it acceptable to add capacity in the process (which itself now comes with new fixed costs). Capacity is equal to the total number of hours you are available in a week (typically 50, for example) times the number of staff members who can perform services independently. If you have 50 hours available that you and a nurse injector are working, then you have 100 hours of capacity. (We won't complicate it here by adding in the capacity of machines needed to do procedures). If you have all of these 100 hours filled all the time you need to raise your price slightly. But this needs to take into account price sensitivity of both your client and the local market itself. With no capacity to fill, you don't look at new customers the same. You need to get higher prices from new customers because with no capacity you really don't need their business.

The other option is to obviously add capacity. But at what point do you add another nurse or another machine? One of the simplest ways to look at this is to see how far out your schedule is booked. If you are booked out 4 weeks and a new machine would allow you to cut that back to one week and would pay for itself within a 2 year period without adding so much additional cost that it made you unprofitable, then you probably want to add this new device. Capacity is also affected by how the length of time a client is willing to wait to get a service. For any consultation that you do not convert that client's business, you need to find out why. If it is because you can't get them in for treatment fast enough, you are effectively limiting yourself by your own capacity. Without actually evaluating your practice patterns, this is a very hard concept to really predict but an extremely important variable to continuously monitor. Just remember that at full capacity you have the lowest fixed cost per service or product that you can have and therefore the highest profit margin possible. Excess capacity costs you money. If you have any difficulty understanding this concept, we encourage you to contact us for clarification.

The first of two exceptions where you would accept pricing changes that are not profitable is when you want to use pricing change as a "loss leader". Loss leaders are those situations when you offer a product or service at a price that you know is at or lower than your actual cost. You do this only in situations where you believe there is something to gain from gain long term from the client. In some cases, this makes sense when you believe that a client, once in the door, will ultimately buy profitable services from you that will more than make up for the difference. In the long run, an example of this may involve performing microdermabrasions at a loss for a patient whom you suspect will become a BOTOX Cosmetic client. The long term revenue you gain from introducing them to BOTOX Cosmetic and/or other facial injectables as well as potentially other more invasive procedures will easily make up for the small early loss from the microdermabrasion treatments.

Another situation where you may use loss-leader pricing is when you are in a situation where you can push a competitor out of the market by being aggressive enough with pricing that they decide to discontinue offering that specific product or service. Market share gives you better control of pricing and the ability to set price increases at dates in the future and move beyond an unprofitable state. But this can also be a very risky strategy because you may start a pricing war that doesn't affect your competitor but instead ends up re-setting market price so low that neither you nor your competition can compete within this specific product or service category.

Intelligent pricing strategies require discipline and not just discipline to maintain pricing you set but discipline to stay in touch with your market, discipline to understand what your profit per client is, and the discipline not to offer discounts unless there is a clear benefit in doing so. Unprofitable growth is not an acceptable business principle. You can be a premium business if you offer premium products and services but even in those situations you must grow profitably through disciplined strategies. In other words, setup a process to deal with price, be disciplined about how you execute that process, and don't guess or assume you understand how elastic the market is or how much your clients specifically value your relationship. Measure it, learn from the measurements, and adjust to make sure you are getting the maximum profit per hour.

CHAPTER SUMMARY POINTS:

- Understanding local price sensitivity is the key to setting an appropriate price point for your goods and services within your specific market.

- Pricing is not a one-time event. Review your prices on a regular basis and don't be afraid to adjust them to meet market conditions.

- Adjust pricing based upon your capacity

- Offer "loss leaders" when appropriate, but be careful not to become the discount provider.

- Unprofitable growth is not an acceptable business principle.

Chapter 16

NON-TRADITIONAL PROMOTIONAL MARKETING

"We don't grow unless we take risks. Any successful company is riddled with failures."

James E. Burke

There are over 300 million people living in the United States today. But even if every one of them had a computer and access to the internet it doesn't necessarily mean that you should have a website for your business. It doesn't mean you shouldn't either. After you have defined who you are, determined what products you want to offer clients, and developed a solid marketing plan and created brand identity (as we discussed in previous chapters), you should now look at alternative marketing concepts such as a website. At its most basic form, a website is a storefront in cyberspace. In healthcare, we don't typically think of a doctor's office as being a storefront but in some ways it really is. Let's start by deciding if you need a website.

Should you have a storefront in cyberspace? Good websites can cost you between $2,500 and $25,000 so you must make this decision carefully. The best strategy is to hire a search engine guru for a single fixed fee project to show you how much traffic there is in your area on the internet for your specific offering of products and services. If there are only 3 searches a day for "Seattle Plastic Surgeon" and another 5 per day for "Seattle WA plastic surgeon", then you may not want to be in cyberspace yet. Look at all the services and products you offer separately because together they may make up enough activity to warrant a website. You also need to analyze competitive websites.

Check for websites from every competitor you have through basic web searches for each of your products and services and you will ultimately identify your competition. We recommend that you only look 2 to 3 pages deep on Google, MSN, and Yahoo. Most other search engines are not mainstream enough to help you understand the potential and anything beyond 3 pages deep is rarely ever seen by a consumer. Be specific enough to get the real story by typing in "Seattle WA BOTOX" and "Seattle Botox" as opposed to just "Botox". In most major cities in America today you will find the need for a website with cosmetics but don't assume, verify. The beauty of an internet presence is that you are effectively open 24 hours per day. There will always be clients who are a little hesitant to just jump in and call you. They want to look through websites and see how they feel about you before making that call or email. But if you aren't on the web, you will never get the call.

Assuming you have now determined you need a website, let's start by comparing your actual physical office with your cyber office. With your physical office space you are first going to look at location because the rule is location, location, location. Location is also critical in the web world but in this case it is location on a particular search engine and location on the page brought up when someone is looking for your specific services. Google is the most popular search engine, but certainly not the only one. And if you can get a first page listing on Google then you are in good shape, right? Usually. But I have seen many cases in my time working with the web in which a website owner said "I'm totally cool on my website because I am number one on Google". Number one on Google means that if someone types in a keyword phrase in a Google search bar, such as Seattle Plastic Surgeon, then your website comes up first. We mean first below the paid websites that occupy the first 3 slots on the top of the page. These practices buy their way there but most internet savvy consumers actually avoid those links. When someone says they are number one on Google I usually ask them for what keywords? They usually don't know because they were shown that they were number one on Google by the Search Engine Optimization (SEO) guru they paid big money to. About that time, I pull up a Google search box and type in "Dry Creek Road Denver, CO Plastic Surgeon" and, sure enough, up pops their website. Now I show them that if I type Denver, CO Plastic Surgeon, their website doesn't show up until page 8. And when was the last time you went to page 8 when you searched for anything? You can be number one on Google for a search engine phrase that no one ever types in, but exactly no one will ever find your website.

The internet is based entirely on the use of keyword phrases. The previous paragraph points out why you must take the keywords you use on your website very seriously. Google, MSN, Yahoo, and other search engines will eventually see your website once you build it and place it on the internet with an appropriate domain name (the name after the www. part). In most cases it takes at least a month for search engines to see your website but there are little tricks that your SEO person can use to make sure you get viewed by the search engines even earlier. When search engines see your site they take a picture of it in a process called caching (your SEO guy is going to call or email you and tell you that you have been "Cached by Google" which means they saw you). Once they have a picture of it, they analyze what your site says. They focus mostly on text you have written, and break it down into one, two and three keyword word phrases and determine if you are selling silk plants or medical services from those specific keyword phrases. You generally should have approximately 5-8% of your keyword phrases mentioned in the text on your site in order for a search engine to recognize you as who you want them to think you are. to be exactly what you want people searching for. For example, if you are a dermatologist offering cosmetic laser hair removal in Binghamton NY, your webpage (each webpage within a website should be treated as its' own entity and optimize separately) should have the phrase laser hair removal on the page at least 5% of all the three word phrases on the page. It really should say Binghamton Laser Hair Removal so that you don't get confused by other areas of the country

Some people have tried to just put two and three word phrases (one word keywords are usually not as important for websites offering specific things) all over their site to attract attention but Google and other search engines see this as spamming your site and they will often ignore you for doing so. In other words you can't just say laser hair removal 100 times in a row or they will reject you. The most important thing when writing copy for your website is that you create a balance between traditional well written marketing copy and the need to make the page search engine friendly. SEO consultants can help you manage this but you are going to have to accept that you're not always going to like what it says in the paragraph because it may not sound perfect. What you really want is for people to come to the site and check you out and ultimately schedule an appointment--because optimization and messaging can often be an arduous task but a task that is nonetheless critical to the success of your online presence.

Keywords also play into the choice of a domain name. Search engines will always favor a domain name that is exactly like keywords typed into the search box. If your domain name is www.atlantacosmeticsurgeon.com and someone types that in the search box, you are much more likely to be on the first page of Google then if you choose www.drbobsanders.com. Domain names cost approximately $9.00 per year from providers such as Godaddy.com. And the web world has a registration process so that no two people can buy the exact same domain name. Don't be surprised if the ideal domain name is not available to you when you actually attempt to buy one. Most of the location and service specific domain names were purchased a long time ago. Hyphens and dashes work better than most people think so you can use www.atlanta-cosmeticsurgeon.com and that will help but it won't be as good as the non-dash version. Having a keyword specific domain name is very important so keep working on it until you come up with something that meets the criteria but doesn't compromise search engine value.

At this point you have decided to build a website and you have purchased a domain name. Now it is time to have the website built by a professional. There are some specific "do's" and "don'ts" to consider.

Do's:

1. Do have a home page based on the highest search service or product you use. Typically this is a general page in cosmetics such as Binghamton Plastic Surgeon. Many people don't narrow down to breast augmentation or BOTOX Cosmetic at first.

2. Do have a webpage for each unique service and product you offer. Internet searchers would choose to land on exact page with the exact information they are looking for rather than land on the home page and have to search for what they are looking for. All of the pages within your website are going to be linked together but most savvy searchers looking for BOTOX Cosmetic injections would rather land on your BOTOX Cosmetic page, get the information they want, and then sign off rather than have you make them click 3 or 4 times to actually find your BOTOX Cosmetic page. You need a simple link on each page to allow the viewer to navigated back to your home page anyway. Linking pages to each other within your website is far better for search engine visibility anyway.

3. Do have a way to be contacted on every page. The worst thing that can happen is that the person looking at your website wants to contact you but can't find a way to do so on the specific page they are on. Provide a Contact Us link on each page. When they go to your contact page, make sure you have easy to understand contact information. If you frustrate them at this point, you have essentially turned away a potential customer at your door.

4. Do make sure you can change the content on your site often. Many website developers will talk you into using a flash only site for a lower cost. While they might look nice, search engines like looking at sites that change reasonably often and flash only sites cannot be changed easily by you or your staff. Changing information regarding new procedures or specials you may be offering is a good example of what you need control of.

5. Do have as many valuable links to and from your site from other highly ranked sites as possible. Examples include, The American Academy of Plastic Surgeons, City Search, CNN or Oprah (if you are really lucky and if you are that lucky please call us). Meaningful links include referring physicians or centers you work with, local media, a link to your own blog (explained later), links to satisfied patients websites, links to news articles that are relevant to what you sell, and links to articles you may write and publish. You need links to other sites and you need other sites that link to you. An SEO consultant can help you with this. Ask every one of your clients if they have their own blog or website. You will be surprised by how many that offer this and they can be very valuable references in your optimization campaign and provide links (and ultimately increased traffic) back to your site.

6. Do make sure every image you put on your site has an alt-tag (this is the little box you see when you hover over an image that comes up by your mouse). These tags are very well liked by search engines and go a long way towards enhancing your overall site optimization. They also help explain to the user what the image is. If there is an image showing blepharoplasty on your site and they think it shows skin resurfacing, you simply won't get your point across.

7. Do put your website in your email signature, on business cards and in your exam rooms in a visible way. If you have computers in your rooms that you allow patients to use while they are waiting, make sure they default back to your website. If you need information from clients prior to their first visit, invite them to go to a specific page on your website where they can fill out personal history and provide the information you will need on the first visit rather than having them fill out the forms in your office. You will look very current to them if you do this. You do of course need a secure page on your site to accomplish this but by doing so you will enhance your search engine position by increasing traffic to your site so

when they fill out the form, send a thank you form with a link back to your site for them to click on.

8. Do put at least one link on each page that calls the viewer to action. Examples include "Click here to make an appointment", "Get our free newsletter here", "Click here to read testimonials from our many satisfied clients", or maybe "Connect to our blog and review our frequently asked questions list". Offering something of value for free has always been a great strategy on the internet. In your case, it should be something informational because that is what most clients are looking for. Free consultations are actually not looked upon as a good idea for Dermatologist and Plastic Surgeons because we are doctors and our professional opinions are valuable. At some point in the process of converting a client from a potential client to an actual client you may in fact give them the consultation for free but you should establish a value to the consultation. For example, you could charge $150 for an initial consultation and then credit this amount to a procedure when they ultimately schedule. It can also be used to negotiate with someone who wants a discount but that can only be done if you set a price up front. If something costs nothing, that something is seen as having no intrinsic value.

9. Do use tracking software on your website. Tracking software allows you to actually see who visited your website. Anyone who goes to your website is looking for something and why not have the ability to contact them afterword and ask if they need help. This has value for the transient web searcher but even greater value when you are sending out emails via a contact manager and having those clients go directly to a page or special on your website that you stimulated them to via the email. In these cases we would recommend that you follow up with a personal email or phone call because they are interested but may have some small issue on why they didn't go forward and book an appointment. It may be they thought the price would be too much and in reality it may not be or they

think they have to pay the whole $25,000 up front and you have a payment plan they can use. If you have capacity to fill this is a great way to find interested potential clients.

Do not's:

1. Do not build a boring website/webpage. Getting people there is the frustrating part, but if you get them there and they don't stick (sticky is an internet term for a webpage that keeps people on the page for longer because it is interesting) then you're not likely to get any business from them. Web pages need to have a fine balance between visual appeal and ease of navigation. Let your 50 year old neighbor play with you site prelaunch. If they can't find their way around, you need to change it.

2. Do not make content so clinical that a layperson can't understand it. As mentioned earlier, search engines look for keyword phrases such as "breast augmentation" or "nose job". While there are a fair number of people who know the word "Rhinoplasty", the vast majority type in "nose job" for the same search. You may not like this but you can either be proud of your content or you can get people to read it. If you want a return on the investment you made in building your website and the recurring hosting fees and maintenance, then you certainly want people reading it.

3. Do not wait too long to react if you are not getting enough traffic to your site. There are more than 50 ways to optimize different aspects of your site to increase visibility. After the initial waiting period is over, keep trying things until you see the progress you need. You can be number one on a Google search one day and on page 3 the next. Things change constantly on the internet, and you need to go with the flow and adjust accordingly.

4. Do not put a link on your site that allows users to navigate away from the site itself. Links to other sites should open a separate pop-

up window for them to look at. To get more traffic, and a higher ranking, you must have more traffic on your site longer. It is a chicken and egg situation. You need more traffic, Google is going to measure how much you get, and you need that traffic to stick on your website as long as possible and Google will also measure that. Links are great. But links that take users away from your site are not.

5. Do not make people buy something or automatically subscribe to something just to get basic information. We like having subscribers to your site that then receive a monthly newsletter emailed out automatically to them through an auto-responder. But that needs to be a passive option to them not a demand. They have to opt-in (an internet term meaning agree to be solicited directly by you) before you send them. A complete overview of auto responders will be discussed in a following chapter.

A large part of the potential return from a website is the result of the growing popularity for the Internet as a resource for information on just about anything. Google's primary mission, as stated in their own literature, is to manage all world wide information effectively. The internet is a very easy place to find information without having someone selling you something. And that is why it continues to grow so rapidly. The reason this is so important to understand in website development, is that while you can have a potential client come to your cyberspace storefront you may never get the chance to sell them on how qualified you are to help them. This becomes far more of an issue when you are promoting products and services that are personal. Cosmetic procedures, products, and services are inherently personal. Find a way to introduce yourself to the viewer and make them comfortable with you so that in time you will have the chance to do business with them.

In surveys we performed, we have found that internet searchers looking for cosmetic procedures or products want to hear the doctor's voice and see his or her picture. We recommend that you feature a short video of yourself talking to a client so that the viewer can feel comfortable enough with you to consider a consultation. If you aren't the kind of person who makes people feel comfortable, consider having a client talk about the quality of your work or even incorporate a staff member. Have your staff review your site and ask them if their first impression is positive or not and then adjust the site accordingly. Deal with absolute reality here. If you don't appear warm and fuzzy on a video, don't put yourself on the video. Make sure your staff gives you honest feedback. There are many examples of advertising in which the doctor is just not camera friendly. Put your ego aside, and you will get more business. If you are great at making people feel comfortable, then get several videos up and running on your site.

At this point, you may have some idea of the cost of a website but you're not sure you know all of the costs involved. Website design, domain names, hosting fees, SEO consultants, maintenance, and content development all vary in cost and quality. Most of your competitor's websites will indicate on the bottom of site who actually built the site. If you like what you see, then make contact with the web designer and get an estimate. Most web designers who build your site know SEO consultants or can do it themselves. I wouldn't automatically use the same group for both critical functions. Many web designers understand HTML (the code language internet sites are written in) but they simply don't know how to make Google happy. Shop around.

These same designers should also be able to build you a Blog. Blogs are generally free unless you want special features, pictures, or other coding work included and are essentially web pages with tools that allow you to easily post new information or viewer comments. They are very important to your overall web strategy because search engines love the fact that this information gets updated all the time. Search engines like new information because it makes them more valuable to the users of that particular search engine. If there is something brand new out there, I want the search engine to find it for me every time I use the internet. We recommend that you have a blog and that you link it to your website pages. And most of the pages on your website should have a link to post something on your blog or allow users to read something from your blog or both. If your blog is linked to your website and you update your Blog, search engines will see the update and then check each link that is connected to that Blog thus getting them back to your site. The end result is that the Blog can help increase traffic to your site and ultimately improve your organic ranking on Google and other search engines.

Last, but certainly not least, (especially in terms of cost) within your internet strategy should be consideration of pay per click advertising. Google, MSN, Yahoo and virtually every search engine makes money by selling advertising to people like you and I who have websites. This advertising appears in several ways. When you first open a page, you typically see 3 websites listed at the very top in blue. All of those sites paid to be in that position. They may be new sites who haven't been organically ranked yet (organically means to be ranked just on the merits of the site without using any paid advertising) and they want immediate exposure. They also may be sites that have been around for a long time but have determined that it is more cost effective to advertise at a price (can be as low as a penny per click or as much as $10 or more). Keep in mind that if you use pay per click advertising, all search engines will charge you a fee whenever someone clicks on your link whether they buy something or not. Using pay per click usually means you can avoid the SEO consultant. But in the cosmetic healthcare arena, expect to pay $500-$5,000 or more per month for this type of service. You will also find pay per click advertisers down the right side of most search engine pages, as well. The higher you are on the page the more it cost you per click. Our recommendation is to hire an SEO consultant but also do incorporate some level of pay per click campaign for this site while you are waiting for search engines to organically rank you. Once you have enough traffic to get organically ranked at a level you want, then you can back off on the pay per click advertising and get your traffic for free.

The internet will eventually affect every business in the world. Whether you develop a website now or wait until a more appropriate time for your market, you will eventually need a strategy. And you can learn as much or as little about the internet as you choose. But ultimately the cost of using it will be affected by how much you or your staff can do versus how much you outsource to designers and consultants. Always look at what your expected return on investment will be with whichever strategy you choose. The road to the internet is littered with money spent by unaware consumers who were sold a number one ranking on Google with a search phrase no one looks at. Don't pay double by making this a secondary strategy and having to do it all over again when it doesn't work.

CHAPTER SUMMARY POINTS:

- Supplement your marketing approach with non-traditional methods such as an internet presence (practice website +/- BLOG).

- Search engine optimization (SEO) is an essential part of your website. But be sure to understand the basics so that you can optimize as effectively as possible. And if you can't do it, get a good company that will.

- Choose your domain name wisely. Incorporate keywords associated with your business and choose accordingly.

- Produce a BLOG and allow your patients to post testimonials or other discussion related to your practice and goods & services offered.

- Last but not least, consider a pay-per-click campaign to drive traffic to your website in the short run. But for long-term results, emphasize overall optimization of your website to improve your organic ranking.

Chapter 17

REFERRAL BASED MARKETING

"I can't believe that God put us on this earth to be ordinary."

Lou Holtz

Over time, successful businesses and medical practices eventually get to the point where they are fortunate enough to either limit or stop spending money on traditional marketing. This happens when they draw enough patients to get all new business from referrals. Your marketing budget transitions from all the traditional methods to one that pays for actual referrals from your existing clients by giving those clients discounts and other incentives. As mentioned earlier, we suggest that practices allocate as much as 10% of their total revenue to their marketing plans. This approach is obviously most applicable for those practices that are new or who need to boost their immediate revenue. Referral based marketing is the technique of attracting high quality new clients through referrals from existing clients or from business relationships you develop. Traditional marketing is a fixed cost that may or may not allow you to tie your cost to revenue received directly from those expenditures. In contrasts, referral based marketing is a pay for performance marketing strategy where you only pay when you actually get a new client.

To perform this type of marketing effectively you must do two things:

- You must have existing clients, staff members or friends that will refer to you.

- You must have something of value to give the people who refer to you.

Once you have these two basic things, you can create a very high quality referral program. Although we suggest that as a new practice, you focus on brand identify first a referral based marketing program should be instituted simultaneously as well because such an effort shouldn't require any additional capital (at least in theory). You do have to ground yourself in the fact that there is always a cost to acquire new clients. It is either through traditional marketing means and a fixed cost or through referral based marketing which is a variable cost only incurred when you actually attain a new client.

Let's look at it financially. You need to start by figuring out what it cost you to acquire a new client. This measurement is one you should do quarterly for as long as you are in business. In fact, there are two measurements every business owner should know off the top of their head:

- How much a client is worth to me financially? (This simply means how much revenue and profit I can attain from an average client? For example, what is the average total revenue and profit you get from a facial injectables client over the lifetime that you serve that client?)

- What is the average cost of acquiring a new client?

Why are these so important? In this industry, there will always be opportunities that come your way that you have to react to as they happen. Many of these require that you can either discount to win new business or buy into a marketing program. Either way, you may not have much time to analyze whether or not this business opportunity will be profitable for you or not. This is why knowing your average cost per client acquisition and your average revenue is critical.

In looking at the cost of acquiring a new client, you must first factor in all of your costs. These costs may include brochures, website costs, advertising in all formats, referral based marketing costs, promotions, and local engagements you attend to interact with people that might become customers. The sum total of these costs divided by the total number of new clients you get gives you your average cost per client. Using a simple example, if you annually spend $10,000 on all forms of marketing and you get 100 new clients, your cost per client acquisition is $100 per client. If your revenue per client averages $2200 and your profit is $1,000 then marketing at $100 is a very good investment depending on your profit target. Figuring out the profit per client in each area was discussed earlier but to reiterate you need to take the total number of clients you perform a particular service for and divide that into the total revenue you receive. Take that revenue per client number and subtract all the variable cost per client that you use and an appropriate amount of the fixed costs and you have a profit per client number to work with.

There are many types of referral based marketing ideas you can use to increase your client base and profit. Start with your staff. We recommended earlier that you treat your staff for free so that they not only receive direct benefits of what your practice does but they will understand the services you provide so they can most effectively recommend them to others. If it costs you $100 per client for acquisition through traditional marketing means then give you staff part or all of that as a reward. In most case $25 or $50 in cash for a referral will be enough to motivate them. If you staff member refers someone for a consultation and they don't end up choosing to be a client then you don't pay your staff a bonus for that. This means you only bonus your staff, which means you are incurring that amount as a cost to your business, when someone they refer actually pays for a service. Pay for performance is the way of the future in many industries and you can use if very effectively with your own staff.

Remember you only pay when you actually get a new client and a new client has a profit level associated with them that you need. With all referral based ideas, you have to keep your profitability per client in perspective. If you perform waxing, for example, and the procedure only yields a lifetime profit of $50 then you don't want to pay your staff, or anyone who refers to you for that matter, $50 in bonuses. This is one of the reasons you must know your profitability per client for every service or product you sell. You will never be able to make decisions effectively without it. We find that paying 3-5 percent of the revenue per client back to someone who refers to you is the best plan. This type of referral bonus works very well in an all elective aesthetic service environment but if you take a mix of elective customers and insurance based customers, especially Medicare, you must consult the Medicare anti-kickback rules before proceeding. It is very likely that you will be able to give benefit to someone who refers to you but Medicare has stipulations that must be followed.

Direct client referrals are easily one of the best means to get new customers. We tend to reward more to clients who refer to us because they generally have a much wider audience of potential referrals and we want to make sure the incentive is motivating. Would you give a free CO_2 laser treatment to someone who referred a client to get CO_2 treatments? It depends. With referrals from other clients we tend to go as high as 10-20 percent of the revenue in one treatment for the referral and in some cases even higher. It must make sense financially against your cost of acquisition of a new client and your profitability per client. In the example above if your total revenue for an average CO_2 treatment is $1,500 and you give a 10% referral bonus credit to your client, which means $150, then you have actually exceeded the cost of acquisition of a typical client if it is $100. That wouldn't make sense to your business. The referral bonus must be equal to or less than the average cost to acquire a client or it isn't a good business decision.

In some cases, you will achieve very high profitability in a given area either due to lower costs and higher revenue products or excess capacity on a fixed asset. In this case, you can incentivize the referral at 100 – 200% of the cost of a single treatment when it involves a high likelihood of multiple treatments for this new client. Laser hair removal, medical skincare products, and in some cases even Liposuction can even fall into this category for example. Generally, if you get a referral for one body part of hair removal and your typical hair removal client uses 6 treatments then giving the referring client a free treatment or two is well within the guidelines of a profitable decision. Be consistently generous and you will consistently reap the benefits.

Another way to attain referrals is to give away free treatments or products to people who are not existing clients but who direct referrals to you. Examples include the receptionist in the lab down the hall, your dentist and dental hygienist, your primary care physician's office, as well as hair salons and day spas that don't offer the services you do. But make sure they don't offer the same services and procedures you do to avoid competition and/or overlap. Treat these people right, explain to them what a good referral is, give them your cards and brochures to hand out, and set up a program that rewards them with complimentary treatments or other incentives as they refer more clients. But be careful not to improperly set their expectations so that they think they can choose from anything on your menu of services. Follow the same logic you would when rewarding clients who refer by giving them a service or services to choose from relevant to the value of the client they bring to you.

Last, but certainly not least, are "bring a friend programs". These can be very beneficial in getting new clients because you promote the idea that if someone comes and they bring a friend with them that both clients will receive a discount on a treatment. With no or very low variable cost services such as Laser, CO_2 or other like devices you are better off getting more volume through a single asset then being concerned about whether you give people a 50% discount or not. If you have 20 slots available this week to treat patients and you can fill two of them at 40% off that is better than getting one at full price. If you don't have capacity and would have to open up more hours just to accommodate the treatment then you are incurring variable cost for the labor and time and you should avoid any discounting programs. Keep in mind that all discounting programs you use, including referral based marketing programs, cannot lower your prices so that you become a low cost provider. One of the reasons is it good to give a service away for a direct referral is that it does not involve a price change. An offer that says "refer a friend and get a service of equal to or lesser value never actually shows up as a specific price change. "Buy 5 and get one free" on the other hand does imply that you are going to take the cost of 6 treatments and reduce it to the cost of 5 treatments while still giving 6 which means you are reducing your price.

The key to success in any business is creating new capacity on a continuous basis and then profitably filling that capacity over and over again. This implies that your schedule will fill up thus reducing the fixed cost per procedure associated with your regular labor hours and equipment. If you can then improve productivity the end result will be that you are now able to open more patient slots using the same amount of labor and technology while getting an increasing number of clients you do in an average week. This lowers your fixed cost per procedure further and drives up your profit. While no one can execute this forever without adding assets you need to find your limits by continuously creating new capacity through better productivity and then filling that capacity profitably through marketing and referral programs.

By implementing a referral based marketing program, you can fill your schedule with new clients at a reliable cost per client. Start your business by building a solid brand identity for quality and high levels of customer satisfaction. Create an effective traditional marketing program and web strategy to gain more clients over time. Once you have gained enough clients you will be able to transition to a referral based marketing program so that all of your marketing dollars are paid out only after you have acquired the new client and received the new revenue associated with that client.

CHAPTER SUMMARY POINTS:

- Referral based marketing (RBM) is one of the most effective means for attracting new clients and involves culling these clients from pre-existing clients or business relationships.

- To be effective, RBM requires that:
  - You have existing clients, staff members, or friends who will refer to you
  - You have something of value to offer them for these referrals

- To evaluate effectiveness of a marketing campaign, be able to calculate its actual cost in acquiring a new client.

- Incentivize your referral sources. No one ever does anything for free.

- The key to business success is continually creating new capacity and then profitably filling that capacity...over and over again.

Chapter 18

DATA BASE MARKETING

"The price of greatness is responsibility."

Winston Churchill

"Would you like fries with that?", "Would you like to buy a CD while you are opening your new checking account?", "While we were changing your oil we noticed that your air filter is pretty dirty and we would like to change that for you also." We have all experienced cross selling and we usually don't care for it. We know what we want and we don't need some kid behind a counter trying to up sell us. Cross selling, up selling, and other techniques have been used for years. Once the internet became a commercial reality, we gained the ability to cross sell at an entirely different level. I am not referring to our ability to perform commercial transactions on a single event basis. I am referring to the ability to collect information over time on our clients, develop an understanding of their demographics, preferences, and buying tendencies and then sell them something they specifically need. We refer to these techniques as database marketing.

Database marketing is an avenue that all practices should use to drive growth in their business. By compiling data that customers give us on patient information forms—e.g.: base demographics related to their age and health—as well as information obtained during consultations and specific feedback obtained during their treatments, we can create targeted profiles

...ey are and what other services they may need. As an example, if ...'re performing skin tightening (perhaps through facial surgery) and ...ur client remarks that they are concerned about hyper-pigmentation, you can easily suggest and market to them a prescription skin cream to get rid of the spots. In this example, you may have the data available to you in the patient chart and you may not. The key to database marketing is making sure it is always available when you have the best opportunity to use it. You should also use database marketing to stimulate your clients to consider special promotions you have as well as to get them reengaged in your business if they have been away for awhile.

To initiate a database marketing plan, you need to do several basic things. Start by making sure you have appropriate database software. Many offices use a software package that controls scheduling and billing. Others have a separate package that just allows for storage and sorting of client data. Because there are so many packages available, at this time we don't endorse any specific one. Whatever database you do use, it will need to have the ability to customize the number of fields of data as well as the types of data you collect. An example of a field of data would be birth date or skin type.

We recommend you collect at least the following:

- Name
- Home/business address
- Email
- Birthdate
- Past Medical History
- Current product use
- Areas of need (e.g.: breast enhancement vs. body contouring vs. facial rejuvenation)
- Short/long-term goals
- Height/weight/body type

In addition, make note of specific preferences (such as life events) that differentiate them from another similar client. For example, if they just had their 3rd child and do not plan to have any more kids, you may propose a "Before Baby Body" type makeover. If they were recently divorced and re-entering the dating scene, that is also important. Many people associate their new single status with the need to refresh their look and you might make a significant positive impact on their transition through this life change.

We understand that you may collect much more information for the client's chart but for database marketing this is the typical data set you will need. A special note on email collection: in most currently available database marketing software, you have the ability to email to a list of people. But this function requires an Opt-In from the client before you are allowed to use it. Opt-In means that you must send the client an automated email to their listed email address and they must click on the supplied link acknowledging that you have their permission to send them emails. This process is important for blocking the practice of email spamming.

Once you have collected a reasonable amount of data, you can then begin the process of segmenting your clients. For example, clients can be segmented by age. While you probably would not offer skin tightening to a 23 year old client, discussing this you're your over 50 clients would be appropriate. On the other hand, segmenting by procedure types can stimulate interest in related products or services. For example, you could designate all BOTOX Cosmetic clients as a procedure type. Whichever database software you choose should be able to filter on multiple data fields at the same time. If you want to identify all female patients in your practice that are over 50 and using BOTOX Cosmetic (so that you can market a filler to them), your software should be able to do that for you. In addition to age and procedure types, you can also segment by specific patient needs. For example, clients who are more than 10lbs overweight and less then 50lbs might be candidates for non-liposuction body makeovers.

The next step in developing your database marketing strategy is assembling the information into usable formats. To do so, there are two areas that you will need to focus on. The first step involves getting the data in the hands of the clinician at the time the patient is in front of them. This process can be achieved by having your staff review the schedule of clients to be seen the day prior to their arrival. A simple print out of relevant information about each client will allow you to discuss potential additions to their current program. The best time to discuss more and do more for your clients is when they are right in front of you.

The next step involves getting information to clients who you are not seeing in the near future. In today's internet world, there are services that provide auto responding to clients. Auto responding is a process where you load client email addresses into one of several available services. Constant Contact and Aweber are examples of this type of service and can allow you to easily broadcast emails to your clients. You take segmented lists you created with your database and load them directly into the auto responder. You then have the ability to format email broadcasts and personalize them to each user automatically (so they think they are the only one getting a message), target them to certain clients, or target your entire client base depending on content. And you can write the emails up to a year in advance and set a broadcast date without even touching it again. These services cost as little as $25 per month and require an Opt-In from your client.

But don't overdo it. If you send your clients an email too frequently, they will think you are spamming them and not pay attention to their emails. Even worse, they will see you as slow and potentially desperate for business. On the other hand, a monthly newsletter that highlights clinically relevant new information as well as products, testimonials, and promotions is probably a good idea. For segmented groups, a stimulating email broadcast once a month is usually acceptable. But these groups should be targeted for the appropriate message at the appropriate time. If you are talking to a client about becoming "bikini ready", you probably don't want to broadcast this message in November. As with all forms of marketing, this approach needs to be thought out and not just done randomly. Messages and grouping should be assembled in a logical manner and test cased when necessary. A good example of poor planning would be where you offer a promotional incentive on facial injectables when you simply don't have the capacity to get new patients in.

The messages you use for database marketing are often different than those intended for traditional marketing. If you are broadcasting messages, you are doing this to people who have given you the permission to communicate with them via an opt-in. As a result, these messages are read more often than not because these people know you and trust you. Don't make your newsletter 20 pages long but also don't be afraid to make it 4 pages long. You would obviously never do that with a billboard promotion, but it is certainly possible with an emailed newsletter. People don't want to read 20 pages of information at one time. Think like a newspaper editor here. On the internet, you will see stories that are on more than one page but not very often because it is well known that the general reader wants information delivered in the shortest, most concise form and not scattered over multiple pages. If it is too long, they simply won't read it. The same is true of email broadcasts. Don't hard sell or over send emails but give your clients information that is relevant to them. If you have segmented properly, the information should be client-relevant. Personalize emails; a good auto responder does a great job of making each recipient think that you are the only one to whom they are sending the message. Tell them you want to confide in them about the results you are getting with a new type of body contouring, facial injectable, or implant (or any other product or procedure for that matter) and how it may benefit them specifically.

And always, always, always give them the ability to contact you back via email or through your website. The worst thing you can do is gain a customer's interest but then frustrate them by not giving them a way to contact you. Include links to your website in every broadcast you send. If your message is related to breast augmentation, link to your breast augmentation page; if the message pertains for facial rejuvenation, you may want to link to multiple pages including medical skincare, facial injectables, and/or laser resurfacing. It is not always in your best interest to send people directly to your home page. Don't make them search for the information they want, connect them to it directly. Each web page of your site should have a prominently displayed "contact us" link so clients can immediately email you to either schedule an appointment or to request additional information.

There is one other data base marketing technique that we recommend that may or may not suit you. Auto responders can tell you (through a reporting function) who opened your email and, in conjunction with your website tracking software, they can also tell you who clicked from your email to your website. This effectively tells you the extent of interest the reader may have in your products and services. From here, proactive businesses will then follow-up with customers who did open the emails and did click through to the website because these select clients actually demonstrated interest. At this point, we recommend that you either call this client or at least send a personal email to them with more information targeted to their specific area of interest. For example, if someone clicks through to your website breast augmentation page and you can tell they actually spent some time on that specific page, you know that you have someone that is probably interested in breast augmentation. And while they may not be 100% interested, you can't afford to take the risk of not contacting them and having one of your competitors potentially get their business. But be careful in your response to the client. Your email back to this client should not tell them that you know that they clicked through to your website. It should have a follow up message from you as a doctor suggesting a consultation or potentially sending them additional patient testimonials for the same procedure. But as good an approach as this is, we actually feel that a phone call is a more personal, and somewhat more effective. Either way, make sure to make contact.

For those clients who do not have access to email, print out a hard copy of the newsletter and make it available on your reception desk along with any current promotions you may have. We don't shy away from mailers but keep in mind that this type of outreach does not have an opt-in component and so you have no real indication of whether or not recipients even read your mail. They are also very expensive relative to database marketing. Sending birthday cards or reminders out can also be a part of your marketing outreach, in addition to using database software to send out e-cards from you to your clients.

Another database marketing concept is to allow combine your efforts with strategic partners. This needs to be done very carefully so as not to offend your clients or make them think you have sold their information to someone else. For example, if you don't currently offer cosmetic dental services, send out a broadcast message announcing that you have now partnered with Dr. Smith (cosmetic dentist who is offering teeth whitening). Including their information in your newsletter and allow them to contribute clinically relevant articles or snippets you think would be of interest to your clientele. And if you are comfortable with it, you can even have your partners advertise in your newsletter or on your email broadcasts by placing banner ads. rough opt-in that they want to receive information from you; they may not, however, wish to receive information or promotional material from anyone else. We definitely do not recommend that you allow partners to advertise or to tag on email broadcasts at no cost. They must compensate you for this privilege in cash or through some other means. They will often allow you to market yourself within their promotional materials to their clients as a reciprocal trade. Either way you are offering your partners valuable access to a list of qualified aesthetic clients and that certainly shouldn't come for free.

Database marketing is a very low cost marketing process relative to many of the techniques commonly used. For as little as $25 per month and a certain amount of staff time, you can contact your entire client base on a regular basis at the same time potentially selling advertising space which may then allow you to recover even more of the inherent cost. If you don't currently use this approach, you are really hurting yourself because it is based on the intimate knowledge you have of your clients and the fact that they trust you. Being a trusted advisor carries with it the responsibility that you will not abuse that privilege; it also carries the responsibility that you be a consultant for their needs. This technique helps you do just that. We will be publishing a separate guide focused exclusively on database marketing for our readers who want more comprehensive and more up-to-date information.

CHAPTER SUMMARY POINTS:

- Database marketing is an extremely efficient way to promote your practice because it allows you to target your client's specific needs.

- Begin by making sure that you have the appropriate software and then identify information fields of interest.

- Email bursts and newsletters are a very efficient way of communicating with your clients. But always allow patients to opt-out.

- Auto Responders are cost-effective and highly effective resources for broadcasting electronic information.

- Always keep your eyes open for synergistic business relationships that will allow you to communicate to a wide audience at the same time providing potential value-added services to your pre-existing client base.

- Never send information to a client about your practice without providing a means for them to respond.

SECTION 6

ZONE OF CLIENT OPPORTUNITY

Chapter 19

CONVERTING WITHIN THE ZONE OF CLIENT OPPORTUNITY (CONVERSION)

"Since most of us spend our lives doing ordinary tasks, the most important thing is to carry them out extraordinarily well."

Henry David Thoreau

Whether you are setting up a new practice or ready to grow an existing one you must now capture more clients within your Zone of Client Opportunity. But which clients? Who are they, where do they come from, and how best do you reach out to them? Some of these key questions were answered in earlier chapters as we discussed the four P's of marketing and your external strategy with clients. But it is very important for you to make sure that you have a strong internal strategy as well. By internal, we refer to what you do when a client comes in the door for the first time and interacts with both you and your staff. The process of turning potential clients into actual clients is referred to as conversion. So how do you convert potential to actual at a very high rate? The best time to win a client's business is when they are standing in your office.

Conversion rates of great practices are generally in the mid to upper 90 percent range. That means that slightly greater than 9 of every 10 clients who inquire about you, call for information about your services, or who ultimately present for a consultation, become your client. To achieve this high a degree of conversion, the first step is to make sure that your staff actually knows what to do when the client shows up. The best practices in America don't let their clients walk up to a front desk receptionist, check in, and then sit down unattended until the nurse or doctor is ready. The best practices know exactly when a new client is going to walk in the door. And when they do, a staff member walks out to the waiting room to greet them, lets them know how long it will be before they see the nurse of doctor, offers them something to drink, and may even spend a few minutes chatting with them. While this may seem very basic, many practices do not do this and ultimately miss a huge opportunity. This first impression is critical in the ultimate conversion of this client. Some practices simply don't do this because it costs them time and money to have a staff member available to meet with each client as soon as they walk in the door. Is this smart thinking? Consider the following. Supposed the average value of the aesthetic client exceeds $5,000. If you pay a nurse $40 per hour and they are waiting as much as ten hours per week to greet potential new clients, you are spending $400 to get $5000 return per new client. The best do it and you should too.

Education of both your staff and your clients is essential in achieving a high rate of conversion. In most cases clients, walk in or setup a consultation with the expectation of solving a problem. And clients rarely know what all their options are for solving this problem. This is where you and your staff come in. As we discussed earlier, you need to have a streamlined consultation process that enables your client to quickly and efficiently identify what problems they actually want addressed. From there, it is up to you and your team to educate them on various potential options available to them. Consider the client who has heard that CO_2 laser resurfacing can improve their skin and make them look younger. While this may be an appropriate option for another client, this client may benefit from a less invasive series of microdermabrasion treatments. While this approach may take longer, it also may be easier for them to endure from the standpoint of discomfort as well as financial outlay. It is your job to get the patient to articulate their problem. From there, then you must educate them on all the various ways to resolve it. They will trust you more if you educate them and let them decide what they want rather than selling them on what they should want.

Another critical aspect of conversion is that your staff must know your product line very well. There are many opportunities in a single visit or a phone call, where a potential client may ask any one of your staff members for information. And although this may come in the form of a direct question, oftentimes the request is more subtle. Regardless, your staff must recognize that questions from potential clients are opportunities. If a client asks, "I saw in your brochure that you guys do fillers, can you solve this problem right here on my face?", a staff member could respond by saying that they don't know and that they will have to ask the doctor. And while that response may be totally appropriate under certain circumstances, your staff could also hand them a brochure describing the various facial injectables, or even have them watch a video loop highlighting your products and services so that they can be educated during their downtime. Your receptionist or staff person who fielded their question should also make a note that goes on their chart as to this particular interest. Very commonly, receptionists or staff members simply assume that a client will bring these questions to you. But many times, they don't. Make sure that your staff are well educated and are not only able to identify an important question, but also address it in the most effective manner. Without doing so, a critical opportunity is lost.

Staff education is also important to prevent dissemination of misinformation to your clients. If your staff under-quotes the cost of a BOTOX Cosmetic treatment, chances are you are going to have a very upset client when they are handed the final bill. If a staff member is asked about the capabilities of CO2 laser skin tightening and they overstate its' capabilities, you will also have an unhappy client. And while some practices choose to have staff members not respond to any customer questions, this approach can also hurt you. In many cases, customers are more likely to ask your staff these important questions than they are to ask you. As such, your staff must be able to engage people at that level and provide good information or the practice will lose valuable conversion opportunities. Spend time each month with your staff going over situations that have come up and review any new ideas that you have about service lines and products so that they remain up to date with the most current information. Discuss any unusual circumstances that have arisen and role play them out. Invest in your staff's education and the investment will eventually reward you with higher client conversion rates as well as higher revenue per individual client.

Don't forget that phone inquiries are important because many potential clients simply can't be sold with a face to face interaction. Phone opportunities may be very difficult to recognize for many people. What makes them so difficult is that in a hectic day when there is a lot going on, many receptionists simply don't take the time to analyze what a caller is really looking for. Never put a caller on hold for extended periods of time. If they have a question about a specific product, make sure there is someone who can take those calls immediately and answer their questions. While this level of response may appear to cost you extra money, considering that each aesthetic client is valued at $5,000 or more and that many become referral sources, investing in resources to drive your conversions higher will eventually produce a substantial long-term return on investment. For every call, identify and record the caller's name so you can easily track their progress and follow up with them. Average medical practices are not focused on this high degree of tracking; great practices are.

Continually measure your conversion rate. Without measuring it, you will never know where you are optimized and where you need improvement. Be able to identify the percentage of clients who came in for an initial consultation and who ultimately purchased a product or service? If your conversion rate is 100%, then you are doing great. But even at 100% you must realize two points. The first is that you must be doing things very well to achieve this degree of closure. The other point is you must realize is that the more consultations you do per unit time, the more business you drive in. So the question is how to acquire more consultations. The answer lies somewhere between the effectiveness of your overall marketing efforts and the optimization of initial contact with your business. To better answer this question, measure the number of people who have called you and track how many eventually came in for a consultation. This is your initial capture rate. From here, you then need to evaluate how many initial consultations ultimately went on to secure paying clients. To be the best, you need to continuously measure to improve and then improve your measures continuously.

Products can and do make a huge difference in your ability to convert potential clients into actual clients. People who want to spend their hard earned money on elective aesthetic procedures will most likely need some level of proof that your service or product line will actually help them. You can tell them all day long how good they will look after augmentation but if they can't personally relate, you're not going to get their business. Testimonials, before and after photos, callable references, and statistical representations of results are all important. The worst thing that can happen to a practice is to offer a product line or service that doesn't produce consistent results for the majority of clients using it. You must be able to show a minimum 90% satisfaction level for any product or service or you shouldn't offer it because it will ultimately create more damage than good. A bad laser treatment that disappoints your client may drive that person elsewhere for their BOTOX Cosmetic, skin tightening, fillers, or potentially an elective surgical procedure. By not offering a substandard treatment, you may a few hundred or even a few thousand dollars of revenue but you also may gain significantly more revenue in other areas when that person refers their friends to your practice or comes back to you for another service. Don't be short sighted on which products and services you offer. You will never be the best at everything, so focus on what you do well and build your reputation accordingly.

CHAPTER SUMMARY POINTS:

- Execution in the Zone of Client Opportunity is critical. To secure the best results, it is critical for your entire staff to execute well not just you.

- Your staff must be highly trained to interact with customers either by phone or in person and they must know enough about what you do to answer questions accurately and to know when it is necessary to hand the client off to you or one of your clinical staff.

- You usually only get once chance at converting a client and so taking advantage of this chance is critical to the long-term growth and success of your business.

- The quality of products and services make a big difference in your conversions. You must assume that you aren't the first provider they have considered and therefore your client will most likely be well-educated as to the differences between various products and procedures. If you are using older, less capable, or comfortable technology expect your conversion rates to suffer when newer technology enters your market.

Chapter 20

DISCOUNTS?

"Great crisis produce great men and great deeds of courage."
John F. Kennedy

The pricing of products and services can be a tricky affair—especially when it comes to discounts. The kneejerk response to a slow schedule or tight economy is to immediately lower prices and offer discounts. But is this the appropriate solution? Generally not. By simply responding to market pressures in a reactive manner, you and your practice lose a great deal of control not only over your current situation but also over future conditions. By responding to slow economic times with discounts, your practice effectively becomes labeled as the discount provider. And while you may not want to be known as the most expensive shop in town, you definitely don't want to be identified as the cheapest. By becoming the local discount provider, you attract a short-term solution. The clientele you bring on board will tend to be the discount shopper. As described in previous chapters, this client is shopping for the commoditized product. As such, quality is not important...price is. And when you eventually raise your prices to an appropriate level for your local marketplace, you lose these people when they gravitate to the next "deal". Short term solution? Maybe. But if you're in it for the long run, I would recommend steering clear.

And so the question is inevitably raised, how do you draw new clients? Is there a way to offer a deal without actually looking like you're offering a deal? Yes. I offer deals all the time; but I refer to them as incentives. I also talk about value-added services. And while it may sound like I am simply playing with language, in reality I really am not. First of all, language does matter. When you treat an injectable client with a filler, would you rather tell that you are going to stick a cc of product in their line or do you gracefully remark that you are going to gently smooth their line with placement of this filler? The end result is the same but the subtle difference in language can elicit an entirely different reaction from your client. The same is true with discounts. By using the terms "free" or "discounts" or "discounted", you are effectively lowering the bar for your clients and telling them that you are worth less than your competition. Instead, choose different language. I prefer to emphasize "incentives" and talk about value-added services. So what is the difference?"

The word "incentive" can mean the same thing as "discount" but has an entirely different ring. To incentivize someone is to motivate them towards an endpoint by offering a positive outcome. In other words, you are driving them towards an endpoint or an action. All in all, this is a proactive approach. Discounts are reactive. You simply reduce your normal prices by a given amount and the client pays less. There is no incentivization here…just a lower price.

In the same way, I like to talk about value-added services. For example, if I need to negotiate price with a Breast Augmentation client, I can do it in one of several ways. First, I can simply reduce my fee and negotiate on a lower price point. While this may seem straightforward, there are long-term effects to this action. If I lower my price now and my competition lowers their price, how low do we both go? At some point, my margin will disappear and I will have no net profit. On the other hand, I can stand firm on my price, offer photos of similar clients (to demonstrate outcomes), offer to have clients who have undergone this similar procedure speak to this prospective client (to enhance confidence in my ability), and I can bundle in another service that this client may be interested in. For example, I may offer to include complimentary skincare treatment to the client's décolleté following her augmentation. Not only will this potentially enhance the appearance of her surgery but it also introduces her to my medical skincare services. As such, this "value added" service has now proactively created not only a breast augmentation client but also a medical skincare client. Value added services can be extremely effective at growing your business and creating long term solutions. Instead of offering a discount and reducing my fee by $100, I have bundled-in this same value and introduced my client to another facet of the business. And now that the skin of her upper chest is smoother and rejuvenated, I have also enhanced the appearance of her surgical results, as well. I refer to this as "Synergistic Marketing". The end result of this combinative strategy creates benefits greater than the sum of the two procedures alone.

The next topic is price point. Setting price point for your menu of products and services can be one of the most challenging aspects of a business. And while you don't want to be the cheapest in town, you also don't want to be the most expensive and price yourself out of the market. Before you decide on what you want to charge, you should first understand what your competition is charging. To do so, call into action your secret shoppers. Have your staff actually call your competition and find out what they are charging. While price points used to be a more guarded secret, in today's competitive environment, more and more practices are disclosing their price scales; some are even going as far as to broadcast them on their website. Once you have an idea of what others are charging, then you need to decide where best to position your menu of products and services. Do you want to compete on price and establish margins through volume or do you want to be seen as a more boutique operation while setting your prices at the upper end of the scale.

Whatever you do and wherever it is that you price yourself, be prepared to defend your decision. My prices are somewhere in the 75th percentile. I have chosen this range because of the type of clientele it provides and because of the practice look and feel that I want to present. If your marketing is Town and Country but your prices are Wal-Mart, there is a disconnect and your clients will be confused. As with every detail in your practice, be proactive and most importantly, be consistent. Don't be afraid to explain why you charge what you charge and stand firm. If a client remarks that you are expensive, offer to show before/after results to demonstrate your results. Emphasize your credentials and make sure that every one of your staff does the same. In working with several secret shopper companies in the last few years, I have always been surprised by the number of businesses in which this does not happen. If the staff that are selling you do not know how to sell you, then there is a disconnect and this will be reflected in your closings. Make sure that the person responsible for these closings is the right person for the job. If they are selling at one price-point but delivering non-verbal clues that don't defend this price-point, your clients will pick this up. Every single one of your staff needs to buy into the notion that you are worth every penny that you charge. Again, defend this through your results, your wonderful long-term relationships with your clients, and your credentials. As we talked about in previous chapters, this is why a focused practice is so much easier to market than a one-stop shopping enterprise. If you can brand yourself as the best person in a specific segment of your marketplace, it is much easier to command a solid price-point for your services. In the past few years, I have focused more and more on breast enhancement and minimally invasive facial rejuvenation to the exclusion of other procedures such as facelifts, rhinoplasties, and body lifts. The end result is that my staff finds it much easier to promote me and to justify my pricing. I perform five types of procedures and I do them well. My goal, and your goal as well, should be to define yourself in your marketplace and set your pricing accordingly. The better defined your services are, the easier it will be to justify your charges.

Again, beware the shopper. Understand what clients you want and then market to them accordingly. Don't expect a Park Avenue practice if you offer the cheapest rhinoplasty in town. As I previously remarked, I am not a big fan of discounts and certainly do not want to be known as the local price gauger. I would rather offer value-added services to introduce clients to other facets of the practice and instill value in the products and services which I perform for them. And be creative. Sending flowers to a client on her birthday will undoubtedly make a much bigger impact than taking $100 off her BOTOX Cosmetic bill. This simple act of kindness can yield dramatic results and create a tremendous amount of goodwill. And it certainly doesn't hurt when her co-workers see a beautiful arrangement on her desk and she comments that it was a gift…from her Plastic Surgeon.

And while these are all good ideas, how can we actually gauge the effectiveness of a specific approach, or more specifically an individual marketing campaign. This is where the "call to action" comes into play. Each and every one of your marketing efforts should be tagged with a specific call to action. This approach can be as basic as a limited time offer or as complicated as the addition of another phone line with the ability to track call volume. Tracking marketing effectiveness overall, can be challenging because many of your clients will come to you after having seen you through multiple channels. For example, someone may hear of you on the radio, check your website, click through to the online yellow pages, and then drop your name at lunch to a friend (who then proceeds to confirm that yes, she went to you and her results are amazing). The end result is that when your front desk asks how she heard of you (and this question should always be asked), she calmly replies that she was referred by a friend. Although her journey began with your radio promotion, you will never know how effective this specific venue was because you didn't tag it with a call to action.

CHAPTER SUMMARY POINTS:

- Referral based marketing is essential to the growth and thrival of an aesthetic medical practice.

- To achieve referrals, you must have:
  - Existing clients, staff members, or friends that will refer to you
  - Something of value to give them for their referrals

- Understand the financial value of each of your clients as well as the cost of acquiring a new client.

- Direct client referrals are always the best type of new clients

Chapter 21

IMAGE & REPUTATION

"Before you can inspire with emotion, you must be swamped with it yourself. Before you can move their tears, your own must flow. To convince them, you must yourself believe."

Winston Churchill

What happens if you spend time and money to build a brand and build the practice itself, and in the end you wind up with a lousy reputation? Although that certainly isn't what you plan for, you must understand the importance of your reputation as an integral part of your brand and you must measure it continuously. Not measuring your image or reputation in the market place is like having a Ferrari that you never check or change the oil on. Eventually all the money you invested in that great car will be wasted because you will blow the engine and it won't work. Your Ferrari may look pretty but it won't do anything for you. In the case of your brand identity and your marketing plan the same is true with regards to your reputation. If you have a poor reputation, you can have that great looking office with very nice brochures and business cards but no one will show up to see them.

Your reputation can be affected by a single negative client reference. In earlier chapters we talked about the value of a single client in terms of profitability. But if that same client is not happy with the service or product that you provided them, then not only will you not lose profit from that

ou will also most likely lose referrals they may have given you. Their
ic complaints can severely hurt you by limiting your exposure to future
otential clients that you will now never get the change to meet. One
negative client reference posted on a blog can be seen by literally hundreds if
not thousands of people. Go into the web and Google "bad plastic surgery
results" or "bad dermatology results" and you will find thousands of entries.

Routinely monitor the web and identify any negative comments or
stories about you as soon as possible. Google your name, your practice name,
your partner's name, and even look for bad results in your market area. Don't
think that just because you are not named that you are in the clear. Guilt by
association may actually take effect and be just as damaging. A quick search
term review on the big three search engines (GOOGLE, Yahoo, & MSN) can
help you identify forums, twitter groups or blogs pertaining to your product
or service. From here, you can routinely monitor them for any negative press.
Make a commitment to check these sites at least once a month and make any
findings a topic of discussion in your monthly staff meeting.

Your staff can also be a valuable asset in monitoring your reputation and
knowing when customers are not happy. Train them to listen for sarcastic
comments made over the phone or in person. Make sure they understand
that not only how to identify these comments but also how to address them.
We probably all tend to have a little too low an awareness level with regards
to things like a client answering the question of how their treatment went
with an "okay". A response of "okay" is okay but it should spark a follow
up question such as, "Is there anything we would have done to make it
better?" Sarcasm may come in all shapes and sizes and can often be difficult
to recognize. So make sure your staff can identify it when it does arise.

Another thing to watch for is the client who consistently cancels or no-
show's for their appointment. After the second one, you should be asking
yourself if this client is truly happy. Most clients are apologetic for missing
an appointment. If they are not, then you need to identify why they are
not. Some clients may go so far as to schedule and cancelling appointments
because they know it hurts your business. These clients need to be politely
reminded that lost time is lost money and that in the future they will need

to secure their appointment with a non-refundable deposit. You need to look hard for client dissatisfaction because for every unhappy client that you know about there are three more that you don't.

And regularly conduct a client forum live with a group of your clients that you trust to give honest feedback. We recommend that you do this no less than twice a year and as often as quarterly, if you can. There is tremendous value in having 10 – 15 clients sitting as a group in your office after hours telling you how they think you are doing. Reward them with a gift certificate to a local retailer or with an incentive on your own products and services for playing an active role in this focus group. Industry has used this technique for years and has labeled it under the term of "advisory boards" or "advisory groups". And you can do the same thing in your practice or day spa. It should just be you and one trusted staff member or outsider meeting with this group so you get honest feedback. If someone doesn't like your receptionist's style in answering the phone or their on-hold time, you want to know that. Surveys can also work for this process but not as effectively as a live question and answer session with the right clients. Take them through your latest newsletter, your website changes, your pricing structure, your new product ideas, and any other area you want feedback on. And review their interactions with your staff and their waiting room experience. This is about your reputation and its contribution to your brand. So don't leave any stone unturned.

When you do find that you have an upset client, act quickly. Call the client and ask them about their concerns and see if you can find an effective way of working with them. Identify their concerns and, if reasonable, deal with the head-on and try to win them back to your practice. The same goes for any negative comments made online. Identify whether or not the comment can be adequately addressed. If it can, then address the concern with a positive spin. If the person is complaining about downtime, talk to realistic expectations and emphasize that each patient is an individual. Interestingly, negative comments properly addressed can actually work in your favor. By doing so, you are seen as a caring physician with insight. You are not only doing your client a service, you are actually helping yourself in the long run, as well. While there will always be clients who are unhappy, in many cases this happens because everyone reacts differently to the same treatment. And each person will probably get a slightly different result. When this happens, your client may feel that they don't end up getting what they wanted. Prophylactically address this with your clients by discussing expectations and outcomes at each and every encounter.

Last, but certainly not least, is the importance of honest feedback from your staff. If you are offering them products and services either for free or at a reduced cost, you should be able to get their feedback on those services as well as feedback on the actual process itself. Encourage them to be critical because you want to be the best and the best deal with even the little things you wouldn't normally complain about. Reward them for their honesty by hosting a discussion with them and attach a small bonus when your measured customer satisfaction rises above your goals. You will spend a significant amount of money advertising, developing a brand identity, and converting potential clients into patients, and you cannot let that money or your time go to waste by not paying attention to what is being said about you. The world has near perfect information access via the internet and there is no reason you can't make sure that your reputation and image are unblemished through diligent research and follow up. Make this a priority.

CHAPTER SUMMARY POINTS:

- Image is everything. Know how others perceive you and understand how to handle both good and bad impressions.

- To do so, you must:
  - Routinely monitor the web
  - Listen to your staff
  - Understand warning signs of the "difficult client"
  - Regularly elicit feedback from your clients

Chapter 22

HIGHLY TRAINED STAFF

*"One can never consent to creep when
one feels an impulse to soar."*

Helen Keller

Everything begins with a phone call. Or in this day and age, it may be an email. However clients first contact your office, they need to feel special. They need to feel as if they are being invited to participate in your services and they need to feel that they are the most important person on your schedule. They should never feel rushed and should never be placed on hold for an extended period of time. As anyone in the marketing industry will tell you, first impressions are everything.

When a potential client calls your office, they decide within the first 15 seconds whether or not they are actually going to move forward and schedule a consultation. If your receptionist is rude, short, chewing gum, or simply not able to communicate how wonderful you truly are, you have lost her. And if your receptionist does not track every single call (which you definitely should be doing) and does not indicate that this person did not schedule an appointment or even ask for more information, then you will never even know that you lost this client.

To put this in perspective, recall the last bad experience you had at a restaurant. You probably did not complain after your meal but swore up and down that you would never go there again. And you told your friends and they told theirs and the reputation of that restaurant was forever tarnished. And the sad thing is that this restaurant may never even know that you had a bad experience...because you didn't tell them. It's the same thing with your business. All feedback, good or bad, is critical in helping you guide your business to success. If you never know where you go wrong, how will you ever be able to make changes?

Jennifer is my front desk receptionist and has been with us for several years. Even on the most hectic afternoons when any reasonable person would lose all sense of sanity, she answers every call politely and appropriately and makes each client feel special. How do I know that? Because I have secret-shopped my own practice and identified strengths and weaknesses. And one of the greatest strengths in my practice is the way in which phones are answered. Using the previous analogy, keep in mind that your practice is like a restaurant and that your client's initial experience with your front desk, or whomever answers the phone or emails, will inevitably determine whether or not that client will move forward and schedule a consultation. Your front desk should know what you do and how you do it better than any of your competition. And you should pay them well for that. Clients can read between the lines and pick up on disgruntled staff members. And when they do, every single dollar that you just spent on branding, marketing, and advertising, is erased. So...keep in mind that it all begins with a phone call.

If you walked into Neiman Marcus and the attendant was wearing faded jeans, flip flops, and chewing gum, you'd probably turn around and walk back out. In less than 15 seconds, you sized up the level of quality of the entire store and their entire image based upon the appearance of a single employee. And if you think this example is an exaggeration, guess again. Your staff are being scrutinized, sized-up, and evaluated every day and with every client interaction. When your staff gossip at the front desk about a client or speak in hushed whispers outside of an exam room (which the client can always hear by the way), they send a negative message contradictory to the positive image that you have spent so much time and energy and money creating. In one second, they have unraveled your efforts and set you back enormously. So what can you do?

While I have not gone to the extreme of uniforms, I have implemented a dress code which states the following. Good personal hygiene in the office is expected and required. Employees must present themselves in a manner reflective of the high level of professionalism we provide our clients. Conservative attire that is generally accepted in a traditional business environment is preferred. The following is not permitted: excessive jewelry, make-up, perfume, denim, attire that leaves a bare midriff or shows too much cleavage, and skirts that are more than 2 inches above the knee. Tattoos and body piercings are not to be displayed. In addition, no snapping or popping of chewing gum is permitted.

Keep in mind that depending on climate and regional culture, dress codes may differ. You will most likely choose to modify this list based upon what is appropriate for your local environment.

Do not be afraid to listen to your staff. Your staff are your eyes and your ears and can keep you out of trouble…if you simply take the time to listen to them. I trust my staff's intuition and appreciate when they politely warn me about a patient who may not have the most realistic of expectations or who may have some type of underlying pathology from which I should steer clear. Gut instinct is more correct than not and I continually look to my staff to keep me out of harm's way. I would rather lose an unrealistic, over-demanding client than deal with them for life. Once you operate on a person, you inherit them…good or bad.

And on the other hand, always listen to your clients. Personality conflicts are bound to occur between your staff and your clients. But be careful to not take sides and to listen to both parties equally. If your staff is at fault, never ever reprimand them in front of a client. Assure the client that you will address their concerns and then do just that. But never do it in front of the client. Doing so simply makes an awkward situation unsalvageable and puts all parties on the defensive. Keep small problems small by addressing them early and appropriately. And as I have fortunately not had to experience much in my years of practice, if a staff member is an inappropriate fit (for whatever reason), do not be afraid to let them go. Each and every one of your staff is a reflection of you…good or bad!

CHAPTER SUMMARY POINTS:

- Your staff are the most important variable in your success. No matter what you spend on marketing and advertising, your staff can make or break you.

- Never forget your staff are a reflection of you…good or bad!

- Always listen to your staff

- Dress codes are essential

Chapter 23

WORLD CLASS CONSULTATIONS

"Success is not the key to happiness. Happiness is the key to success. If you love what you are doing, you will be successful."

Albert Schweitzer

Who is right? In the case of a patient's perspective on whether or not they got more than, less then, or exactly the amount of value they expected depends entirely on what their expectations were upfront. Up to this point, we've focused primarily on how you, the practitioner, can most effectively interact with clients. We've discussed expectations and suggested various approaches for optimizing the physician-client interaction. But until now, we really haven't talked about the patient and delved into their thought process.

There are two primary things to consider in working with patients. The first is how they are managed through your office and how they interact with your staff and the second is how you manage and deliver on their expectations. In the first case, you have to really think about the image you are presenting to patients. If you are a premium provider of aesthetic services, the client experience matters a great deal…not only the outcome they realize from the procedure but also the outcome they see through the entire experience. As such, the critical foundation for a positive patient experience is the world class consultation. And this consulting process does not begin when you, as the practitioner, first walk into the examination room. It begins with the first phone call, the first email, the first contact that the client has with your office. If your prospective client doesn't have a positive experience at this level, you'll never even get the chance to get them into your office.

In conducting interviews for this book, patients pointed to their experience in the waiting room as well as in the treatment room to be a big factor in their assessment of the overall "experience". Their feeling is that if they are going to pay you their hard earned money to have a procedure costing thousands of dollars or more, they want to feel special. One client remarked that when she went to the office of one of our competitors she was "…made to wait for 30 minutes before anyone even said hello to me." She rejected that provider immediately after the initial consultation because she felt that "…if they can't treat me like I am important enough to get to me quicker then that when I am not a patient yet then how will they treat me if I have a follow up problem and I have already paid?"

If you don't currently have someone greeting clients within the first couple of minutes they arrive, then plan on reducing both your overall conversion rate as well as your profit margins. Each and every client should be treated like you would want to be treated. I expect outstanding service from my tire guy let alone someone I am paying money to for something I want not necessarily need. This same scenario holds true for the time they spend waiting in the treatment room. Make sure that any time a client is waiting, that one of your staff have talked to them at the beginning of their wait and have made sure they don't need anything. Offer them something to drink, access to a computer, and give them high quality product and service materials that educate them about your various products and services. Do not let them sit and wait and think only about how much this is going to cost them or let them talk themselves out of it. Pay a visit to Nordstrom's and ask them about their service philosophy. Do the same thing at a Ritz Carlton. Those companies do it right and you can too.

To best meet your client's expectation, you need to think like a client. Understand their goals and expectations and make sure that you are both on the same page. Realistic expectations are the foundation of a strong and successful physician-client relationship and form the basis for the entire future you will share with this client. Keep in mind that once you have performed a procedure for a person, you have proverbially inherited them for life—good or bad! So why not start out on a good footing and maximize the relationship.

The first step involves assessing why your client is actually seeing you. And while this may seem straightforward, very often it is not. While you may think that they are simply seeing you for a BOTOX Cosmetic injection to treat wrinkles, in reality they may be looking for affirmation that there is something you can do to stave off the aging process they are now seeing as they enter their 40's, 50's, 60's or beyond. The ability to read between the lines is one of the quintessential talents of the effective aesthetic practitioner. If practiced well, your relationships with clients will flourish; if not, misunderstanding can lead to dissatisfaction and even worse. First and foremost, make sure that you and your client are on the same page.

The next question your client is thinking (and they may or may not ask you this) is what happens if they don't achieve the outcome they paid for. This is a very tricky area. I learned early on to never guarantee outcomes. Everyone is an individual and responds differently to products and services. And while their friend had a great result with 30 units of BOTOX Cosmetic, they may require 50 units or more to achieve a similar effect. I emphasize to patients that while I generally achieve consistent results, there is a certain degree of variability inherent in each and every treatment as well as with each and every individual person. Your photos and testimonials, while extremely effective at displaying home runs, should also be seen as your best results and not implied guarantees. On the same note, while you should never be afraid to promote your accomplishments, keep in mind that hyperboles (such as claims that you are the "greatest" or the "best" in any one area) can often trap you. If your results do not turn out perfect, these claims can actually be used against you in the court of law when the opposing attorney compliments you on being the "best" in this area but follows by asking how such an expert, like yourself, could ever achieve such an outcome. So be careful with what you say. Promote yourself…but be realistic.

And so we return to the question of how to deal with results that are not what your client anticipated. Unfortunately, there is no easy remedy to this and so every case really has to be addressed on an individual basis. Suffice to say, the answer really originates from your underlying practice philosophy. If you are simply a "churn and burn" factory making numbers off of volume, then you probably don't care; you'll probably also not be in practice very long either. But if you are truly concerned about the welfare of your clients and concerned with your reputation, you will do everything realistic within your power and within the scope of your ability to make it right for every client. An interesting phenomenon that I have found is that while I do not see a lot of complications, for those patients who have had complications or even those with less than anticipated results, when I responded in a caring manner to them and expressed to them that I would see them to the end and do everything I could to achieve a more satisfactory result, they actually turned out to be tremendous cheerleaders for my practice. They were able to see beyond results of their initial treatment and identify that I, and my staff, were genuinely interested in their well-being and didn't simply see them as another client. So is this just a lot of feel good medicine mumbo jumbo? I don't think so. In fact, if it is then I like that mumbo jumbo because it is one of the key essentials that has helped me build a highly successful practice within a very short time. If in doubt, always practice the Golden Rule and treat your clients as if they were you or even a family member. If you do that, you'll never go wrong.

I individualize my approach to any patient that has a less than optimal result. If their expectations are unrealistic and if they want you to accomplish something that you cannot, you need to tell them so and you need to tell them early. If you do this and they still have unrealistic expectations, you need to set boundaries and you need to be clear about what you will do for them. If their outcome is the result of suboptimal correction (e.g.: using too little product), then you need to be honest and directly tell them so.

Realistic expectations are the foundation of a successful aesthetic practice and must be established in the first interaction with every client. I discuss with my clients two things: what I can do and what I cannot do. Each are equally important and, left un-discussed, can lead to confusion, disappointment, or even worse. As such, I am careful to be candid in my initial assessment of the patient. I first ask them what they would like to accomplish and why. Underlying motivations are important as they often provide a window into the inner workings and goals of your new client. Improper motivations are a setup for failure and should be identified from the start. If a patient is choosing surgery, a procedure, or even a product, and they are not doing it purely for their own ends (e.g.: someone else is telling them that they need to do it), they are doomed to failure. This type of patient is going into the session unconvinced that they even need to move forward. The likelihood that they're actually going to be pleased with their outcome is very low. The initial consultation is a chance for this potential client to meet you and feel comfortable working with you. It is also a chance for you to decide whether or not you feel comfortable with the patient. You're entering a relationship, of sorts, so pick your partners well.

Successful outcomes begin with open lines of communication. Setting expectations appropriately is the first step. The next step is an honest discussion of downtime. Every client should clearly understand anticipated downtime. Emphasize to them that while you can speak in generalities, you cannot guarantee down to the minute how much downtime they can actually expect. Downtime is a complex phenomenon which I find difficult to pin down. To some patients, it is defined by the time they need to be in bed while to others it is the duration that they are going to feel any discomfort whatsoever. To others it is the time it will take to totally return to normal (e.g.: no bruising, swelling, sutures, or physical limitations). Address all of these concerns in your discussion with your patient since you won't know which is most important to them. It is critical that both you and your staff understand how each specific patient defines this term. By doing so, you can then discuss appropriate expectations and outline a course of healing that will be both realistic and acceptable to the patient. Understand that the terms healing time and downtime are often used interchangeably and that there are often multiple factors (including ethnic and geographic variations) that often play into each client's understanding and acceptance of each.

The next question is the cost or what I like to call "financial outlay". Very few people walk into your practice with a blank check no matter their financial situation. So clearly define for them what they can expect. I break down my price estimates and let the client know how the final figure is arrived at. For surgical procedures, emphasize that these are merely estimates and that while your professional fee will not vary, they could be charged for additional time by the surgery center and anesthesia if the procedure takes longer than anticipated. If you do not cover this before surgery and you do go over the allotted time, no matter what outcome is achieved the potential is high for an unhappy patient.

How much will this hurt? "It won't hurt me a bit!"…sorry bad joke but it often lightens this part of the consultation. I am truthful with my clients. I do everything in my power to make them comfortable but there is only so much that I can predict and only so much that I can control. Pain is a very personal issue affected by a myriad of variables (only some of which you can manage). If surgery or a procedure is going to hurt, I am honest and prepare them realistically for both the initial discomfort as well as any anticipated discomfort following the procedure.

"What will my family and friends say?" "Can you not tell my husband I am doing this?" In this day of HIPPA rules and regulations, in many ways this is actually easier. If your client does not want someone to know, you are bound by law to not tell them. There is also a level of concern that many patients have regarding how their friends and family will interpret not only the outcome of the procedure but also the underlying motivation for it. They may be afraid that they will be seen as vain, superficial, or even frivolous. They may even be criticized by family members for spending money. You need to address these concerns and even be able to identify them without the concerns ever being raised. Before you perform a procedure, you need to feel comfortable that the patient will be accepting of the outcome. While that may sound like a no-brainer, many people never consider this before moving forward and later find themselves in an uncomfortable position…even with a good outcome.

"Is there anything more that you would do?" Chances are that if your results are good, you will hear this question more and more. But interpreting what the client is actually asking you and being able to answer them is often more difficult than you might think. Many clients are so satisfied with your treatments, whether surgical or non-surgical, that they will be interested in moving forward and addressing other areas. This is a very positive thing and can be highly beneficial in helping you grow your practice. But be careful about the consummate plastic surgery client who does not know when to say when. A mentor once told me that the most important but least frequently uttered word by a Plastic Surgeon is the word "no". I believe this to be true. If your client does not need a procedure, don't recommend one. Client relationships are developed over time and are based on trust. If your client ever feels that you are taking advantage of her by overselling products or services, this trust can quickly erode. The same holds true of the over-doer. Some clients simply don't know when to say when. This is where you come in. You are ultimately responsible for guiding the patient in a direction that will not only be beneficial in the short run but, more importantly, will provide lasting benefit for them in the long run. As such, your role as a gatekeeper cannot be overemphasized.

CHAPTER SUMMARY POINTS:

- The world class consultation is the foundation for a positive patient experience and begins the moment that the client first makes contact with your office.

- To meet your client's expectations, you must think like a client.

- Always consider how the patient views you and your staff. Their perspective may or not may be similar to yours and will ultimately shape the direction of this and subsequent encounters.

- Always keep in mind:
  - How patients are managed through your office
  - How you manage and deliver on their expectations

- A patient's experience is everything!

- Always treat your clients as you would want to be treated.

- In designing promotions or incentives, always think like a client.

- Speak less and listen more. Successful outcomes begin with open lines of communication.

- Try to understand at the initial consultation, why this client is really seeing you.

- Have a back-up plan for addressing patient expectations when things don't go as planned.

- Manage expectations at the first encounter. Realistic expectations are everything.

- First and foremost, never forget that long-standing client relationships are built on trust, require effort, and strengthen over time.

- If you have any questions about the customer service experience, refer to Nordstrom's and Starbucks...they created it!

SECTION 7

PUTTING IT ALL TOGETHER

Chapter 24

YOUR ULTIMATE GOAL - THRIVAL

"Winning is not a sometime thing. You don't win once in a while, you don't do things right once in a while, you do them right all the time. Winning is a habit. Unfortunately, so is losing."

Vincent Lombardi

While the average business seeks to survive, the best look to thrive. And from this, the best-case scenario is a state of "thrival" where your business not only succeeds, but it does so with continued growth and prosperity. And that is the goal of this text. "Simply getting by" is as useless a phrase as "breaking even" and should always be seen as such. Your goal should always be to take your business to a place where you are growing each year and where, more importantly, you are also having fun doing so. Because work enjoyed is not work, it is a career. The more you enjoy what you do, the more infectious that passion becomes. And the more passionate that you are, the more you attract clients from the sheer energy of your enthusiasm. On a social level, most people tend to gravitate towards positive people. The same can be said of a business. The more positive energy you exude, the more clients you ultimately draw towards your business.

And when you achieve a state of thrival, you realize what we refer to as Continuously Growing Profitability. Again, you are never seeking merely to survive; you are seeking to dominant the marketplace and grow your business on a regular and continued basis.

As you've seen in this text, growing your business is not a matter of simply being busy and having a lot of clients…it's being profitable and having the right clients. You learned the basics of your trade in medical school and residency but were never given the keys to implementing your skills. Continually raise the bar for yourself and your practice and the outcome will be consistent growth and prosperity.

CHAPTER SUMMARY POINTS:

- While the average business survives, the best seeks to thrive. And "simply getting by" is never an acceptable option.

- Be passionate about what you do and the energy of your positive outlook will inevitably be contagious. No matter what you spend on outreach, you alone are the best marketing to potential clients.

Chapter 25

WHAT IS YOUR TRUE RETURN ON INVESTMENT (ROI)?

"Great spirits have always encountered violent opposition from mediocre minds."

Albert Einstein

One of the most difficult things about running your own business is knowing when to say yes and when to say no to business. It is a competitive world out there and the beauty business is about to grow at a very rapid pace. And the faster it grows, the more people are going to get involved. Many of those current and future competitors are going to make unpredictable moves with pricing and packaging and to effectively respond or even be proactive, you must know what your return on investment is for every type of product and service you offer.

In most cases, when we review the financials of an elective cosmetic service, we find a financial situation entirely different from what we initially assume. To illustrate this, a recent client was asked what their most profitable service was. In order they said BOTOX Cosmetic, Laser Hair Removal, and CO2 laser resurfacing. When asked them why they chose those three, their response was very revealing and actually representative of one of the most common misconceptions among directors of an aesthetic enterprise. Because there is no technology to depreciate and procedures take

- 185 -

very little time, BOTOX Cosmetic tends to be associated with a relatively high ROI. Laser Hair Removal was chosen because this specific clinic does a lot of it and is are very good maintaining high productivity. And finally, revenue from CO2 laser resurfacing also tends to be high although the capital expenditure is high and the procedures are associated with longer treatment times. And so while these observations where, for the most part, logical on their part, their actual financial results don't necessarily support their initial assumptions.

In reviewing their books, we found that 18.7% of their business is CO2, 13% BOTOX Cosmetic, and 34.9% Laser Hair Removal. From a return on investment perspective the CO2 unit cost $80,000 and if you use straight line depreciation over 5 years you get $16,000 per year in depreciation costs which gets distributed over the 190 procedures done during the year. That means a fixed cost of $84.21 per procedure. Add to that a technologist to run the device at $25/Hour. The total hours used for the year on CO2 procedures was 285 hours for a total labor cost of $7125.00. That number distributed over 190 procedures is equal to an additional cost of $37.50. This brings our total cost per procedure, without overhead, to $121.71. The total revenue generated by the procedures was $118,697 or $624.72 per procedure. Completing the process you net $503 ($624.72-$121.71) per procedure in profit. Looking at in one finally way that is very important we take the net profit from doing CO2, $95,572, and then divide that by the 285 hours of time we yield $335 an hour in profit.

Profit per hour is important because it is the easiest way to measure your best return on investment. We also looked at BOTOX Cosmetic in this same location and determined that they made $241 per hour in profit. The cost of laser hair removal is $22 per procedure including equipment and labor but the net profit is only $274 per hour. What this tells us is that BOTOX Cosmetic is the lowest profit of the three per hour and that they should be emphasizing CO2 laser resurfacing above everything else. In a 40 hour week you can expect to make $3,760 more doing CO2 then you can BOTOX Cosmetic work.

It may seem relatively simple, but it is necessary for all facilities to do their own analysis for several reasons. These numbers may be completely different than yours if you are working with used equipment, receiving bundled discounting or incentive pricing on your facial injectables, or charging much higher prices for your Laser Hair Removal. The one thing you must do to compete effectively and get the return on investment you deserve is to perform this calculation frequently. If you don't know your profitability per hour per service then how will you know what to discount to gain more volume? And what if a client wants a discount on BOTOX Cosmetic but they also use your CO_2 service? Your financial situation may be much further ahead if you offer a discount of 25% on the CO_2 service if someone signs up for a one year BOTOX Cosmetic program. The only way you can make that decision is if you know your profitability per hour.

Capacity is a critical element of this equation as well. Return on investment per hour per service is important but not as important as return on investment for your entire business. Getting ROI for your business depends on the mix of products and services you sell and the capacity to these services. If you are using a nurse injector to do your BOTOX Cosmetic injections and you focus on CO_2 and other surgical procedures you have more capacity because you aren't doing all the work yourself. When you as a practitioner are not busy full time you want to make sure that you do as many of the procedures as you are qualified to do on your own to lower your cost per procedure. It is however critical to keep in mind what rooms, technology, and staff you have available at all times before you promote a service or give a discount. If we could do 55 hours of week in CO_2 business, in the example above, with one unit and the only two people we have on staff to do it, we would stop doing BOTOX Cosmetic all together because of the profitability difference per hour. This changes when you have multiple people and technology sets that each have their own capacity. If you have the capacity to do more work in your practice, make sure you know which work you want more of based on profitability per hour first then look at technology, and staffing issues.

CHAPTER SUMMARY POINTS:

• What you take in is less important than what you take home.

• Knowing what your profitability per hour is for each of your services is critical to developing and adjusting your best ROI strategy.

• Your ROI strategy is more important at the business level then the service/procedure level. Balance procedures and capacity against each other to determine the right mix.

• Competition will force you to react and sometimes react much quicker than you would like. Always knowing first hand where your profit comes from will help you negotiate in an intelligent way to protect your interests.

• Keep up to date on changing profitability. Market conditions can rapidly impact profit per hour on any service; at a minimum, you need to monitor this on a quarterly basis to assure you negotiate and shape your mix with current information.

Chapter 26

PUTTING IT ALL TOGETHER

"I long to accomplish a great and noble task, but
it is my chief duty to accomplish humble tasks
as though they were great and noble."

Helen Keller

By building your framework and incorporating a disciplined monitoring and execution process into your strategy, over time you will develop a profitable business. For most business owners the next question is what can be done to profitably grow their business even further. The US economy grows at approximately 3% on an annual rate over time. To maintain your lifestyle and your market share, you must grow at a rate equal to or greater than 3% on average, as well. Anything less than a 3% growth rate means you are losing market share and losing share is a strategy that always leads to catastrophic failure over time if changes are not made. Grow or die is a common business concept which holds a great deal of truth.

Slow growing economies, like we see here in 2009, can make it especially challenging. Because many other specialties slow when the economy slows, they eventually turn to cosmetic procedures to try and maintain their own revenue and lifestyle. One of the most positive aspects of today's economy for the cosmetic elective practice is that traditionally consumers spend more money on beauty and beauty-related services between the ages of 50 and 70 than at any other time. The baby boomers represent a block of consumers equal to approximately 72 million people currently between the ages of 44 and 64. And we are really just beginning to see the purchasing power of the baby boomers as they drive the demand for cell phones, laptops and the internet to stratospheric levels and as they enter the aesthetic market. Get ready to grow and you can take advantage of a decade or more of very positive business growth in this market.

There are two things you must do to grow and grow profitably. You must create capacity and you then must fill it profitably. Creating capacity means you must improve your productivity. The best case scenarios for productivity growth are also approximately 3% per year which means that if you are growing at 3% per year and increasing your productivity at 3% then you are creating just enough capacity to grow at a rate that sustains your market share. While that equation will prevent your death as a business, it won't necessarily insure the lifestyle you want to live. If you grow at more than 3% and you only increase your productivity by 3% then you must create capacity by adding resources (assuming you are at capacity today). Adding resources can mean simply staying open longer (which means you will be paying staff overtime at a higher rate) or working more hours yourself which means you will be decreasing your quality of life. The other option is to add people and/or technology to produce more capacity. Adding resources must occur at some point in any growing business, but we don't want to add resources until we know that we can profitably fill the use of those resources and we certainly don't think you can sustain working 20 hours/days yourself for very long simply to gain additional capacity.

There is no magic equation for adding 20% new capacity and for actually filling it. This process takes planning and execution along with creative marketing to insure that you don't have new excess capacity for very long. As an example, you may decide to add a nurse injector to perform BOTOX Cosmetic injections for you because you are losing clients who don't want to wait for you to get them on your schedule. You know if you add this nurse you can make 60 new BOTOX Cosmetic injection slots per week. You also know that you can fill about 10 of those slots and generate an additional $2500 per week in revenue. That equates to a net loss of over $500 per week by adding the nurse (See Table 26.1 below).

Nurse working hours	40
Hourly rate	$40.00
Benefits @26%	$10.40
Total Costs	$2,016.00
Botox Cost/Unit	$6.00
Botox used for 10 patients	250
Total Botox Cost for 10 patients	$1,500.00
Total overall costs	$3,516.00
Cost per patient	$351.60
Revenue	
10 patients at $12/unit	$3,000.00
Net Loss	-$516.00
Net loss per patient	-$51.60

Table 26.1

With this said, the minimum number of BOTOX Cosmetic treatments she must perform to breakeven in this equation is 12. But since no one really wants to break even, we really need to do more than that to make this venture profitable.

One of the ways you could potentially overcome this shortfall is to institute a BOTOX Cosmetic referral program right before adding this nurse. During the response to the special, you may end up working more hours than usual to cover the response but that should be temporary. The point is that by adding resources you are effectively creating capacity but you are also adding to your fixed costs. Since fixed costs are distributed over the total number of procedures you do, if you raise your fixed costs but do not add enough new business to cover these costs then you actually reduce your profitability.

When you make the decision to create capacity, you must rapidly and effectively fill it at least to a point of breakeven or you are hurting yourself. So how do you make sure this happens? You do this by planning for the increase in resources and you make sure that you are filling the funnel we showed you in chapter 20. You also need to make sure that client conversion for this category of resources you are adding gets special attention. For example, you would not cover your new fixed costs for BOTOX Cosmetic by improving your Breast Augmentation conversions. You need to excel at client conversions in this specific Zone of Client Opportunity while paying special attention to new capacity before it actually happens. You may want to run a special inside your Zone of Client Opportunity on BOTOX Cosmetic. You may want to contact clients who entered your Zone of Client Opportunity for BOTOX Cosmetic but ultimately weren't converted and then go after these potential resources now that you actually have the capacity. There are a number of good ideas that you can use in this instance but the main point is that you need to do something before you actually add the resource.

Many practices make two mistakes in their quest to create and profitably fill capacity. The first mistake is to create capacity (by adding new resources) before they are operating at maximum efficiency with the resources they already have. If you don't know how to assess your productivity level and efficiency, get help from an outside source. We would be happy to evaluate your practice or refer you to someone else who can. In this, pay for performance is the norm but if you dramatically increase your profits, it is money well spent. This type of input should never be a onetime effort. A consultant should be able to show you how to increase efficiency and capacity now in addition to helping you implement processes that will allow you to do the same thing as you add resources down the road. Adding resources to a bad process or simply maintaining inefficiency will actually increase your loss per resource deployed. When you have inefficiency, effectively multiplies as you add more resources.

A second common mistake is to add resources and then turn up the heat on marketing plan to fill these resources. You need to do just the opposite. You will know when you are operating efficiently and when you are getting close to capacity. When that happens most people take a deep breath and think to themselves, "wow we are really busy and I don't need to spend more money and time on marketing right now". That can certainly allow you to bask in the glory of a very efficient business with a full schedule and growing revenue. But you may at this point miss a very good opportunity to make your business grow even more profitably. If you are full and efficient it means that your brand is strong, your process is effective, and your execution in the Zone of Client Opportunity must be reasonably good. It also means you are getting solid referrals. With more satisfied clients, you can reasonably expect that you could make a big leap forward in growth. While there is no guarantee that you will grow at an even faster rate in the situation described above, there is an absolute guarantee that you won't grow faster or more profitably if you just sit back and take a breather at the moment of your greatest efficiency.

You must prepare your business to grow profitably if you actually plan to grow profitably. Doing that means that you have to use marketing effectively when you are in slow growth markets, normal growth markets, and fast growth markets. Doing that requires you have a high level of awareness of what works and what doesn't work. You create that awareness through measuring marketing performance continuously and making appropriate adjustments to your strategy. No marketing program should ever be run without having a means with which to measure its performance. Track web hits on your website. Track the number of people who respond to your ads. Record your referral sources and reward them well. Above all, utilize calls to action to track effectiveness of your marketing efforts and adjust accordingly.

You will continuously grow your business in a profitable way but you must have the training, efficiency and discipline to do it. You cannot build new capacity and just expect new business to show up. A Field of Dreams strategy doesn't work when you open your business and it won't work when you try to continuously grow your business and maintain its profitability.

CHAPTER SUMMARY POINTS:

- The baby boomers represent a growth opportunity unprecedented in the cosmetic elective aesthetic industry and your business must grow to meet that demand.

- To have a continuously growing profitable business you must improve your productivity at a minimum of 3% per year.

- With productivity improvement and efficient processes, you can create capacity. It is bad business practice to create capacity through the addition of resources when you are not running at maximum efficiency.

- When it is time to create capacity, create demand through increased marketing and through targeted focus in your Zone of Client Opportunity. Waiting to create demand after you have created capacity ultimately reduces profit.

- You need to market in all growth and non-growth markets. The best practices grow even in down markets.

EPILOGUE
STEPPING FORWARD

*"It is not the critic who counts: not the man who points out
how the strong man stumbles or where the doer of deeds
could have done better. The credit belongs to the man who
is actually in the arena, whose face is marred by dust and
sweat and blood, who strives valiantly, who errs and comes
up short again and again, because there is no effort without
error or shortcoming, but who knows the great enthusiasms,
the great devotions, who spends himself for a worthy cause;
who, at the best, knows, in the end, the triumph of high
achievement, and who, at the worst, if he fails, at least he fails
while daring greatly, so that his place shall never be with those
cold and timid souls who knew neither victory nor defeat."*

Theodore Roosevelt
Citizenship in a Republic,"
Speech at the Sorbonne, Paris, April 23, 1910

In writing this book, I have had the pleasure of sharing my tips and pearls with you but have also learned a great deal about myself and my practice in the process. I learned that to build your business, you must first build yourself. A business is a vision implemented in strength relative to the strength of the person or persons behind it. As such, everything you do to improve yourself will be reflected in the character of your practice.

Your internal framework is the seed from which your business grows and ultimately the most important variable in the success of your business as well as a contributor to personal fulfillment. As such, personal discovery should be an integral part of your daily life. The better you know yourself, the better you can build your business and the better you can serve your clients. A business without character is a business doomed to failure. And so you, as the foundation, should provide this character in every way you can.

To do so, strive on all levels to be the best person you can be. Achieve your benchmarks but keep setting the bar higher. No one has ever become successful by doing a mediocre job so ignore "what if" and focus on "no matter what". To capture opportunities as they arise, remove your personal filters. Everyone one of us has biases and perspectives that limit what we see. But these filters only stymie us and prevent us from seeing the true landscape around us. Filters are the greatest contributors to missed opportunity.

And avoid "limiting beliefs". If you think you cannot do something, chances are you won't. Visualize the person you want to become and the business you want to grow and do so every day. Repetition is strengthening; when told something enough times, this belief becomes our reality. In the process, keep your vision and always focus two steps ahead. Most importantly, avoid getting bogged down in the minutiae.

There are "dreamers" and there are "doers". Without the dreamers, we would never create; without the doers, there would be no execution. Your business needs forward movement. Too often, we get caught up in the planning stages constantly reworking our ideas until one day we realize that we haven't accomplished a single thing. A careful balance of planning and action is essential. As you move forward, it's critical not to get stuck. Take action and get out of your own way.

And as you navigate this challenging economy, understand that hard times provide the greatest opportunity to hone down your business, trim the fat, and focus on what's important. Be persistent and be consistent. And once you are successful, never apologize for your success. If you run a business, why not make it a successful business?

If I were to do it over again, I would have done it differently. In the early stages of my practice, I was continually looking for answers when I should have looked for perspective. With proper perspective, you can always arrive at the right answer. And I would have learned more from my mentors. Why reinvent the process when somebody else has already done it? When you learned to ride a bike, you had a teacher. Whether it was your father, your mother, siblings, or a friend, they shared their experience with you and taught you what to do and what not to do and how best to ride a bike. It would have taken you a lot longer to successfully ride without their help. So why should your business be any less important? After a great deal of learning what to do and what not to do, I now realize the importance of modeling myself after mentors who have achieved what I wish to achieve. Keep in mind that time is money. The fewer mistakes you make, the faster you ramp up your business and the quicker you realize the fruits of your labor.

This book has been a journey. I thank you for taking it with me and hope that my experience can prove helpful to you as you enter the business of aesthetic medicine.

Gregory A. Buford, MD FACS

What's Next

You invested in the book and read it. So what's next? In order to make the most of this information, we suggest that you take some very specific steps.

1. Carefully evaluate your current branding. Set up an invitation-only open house for twenty people and invite a good mix of both existing clients as well as potential new clients. Then, have these people participate as a focus group to evaluate specific areas of your practice. Show them your website, your collateral material, and any other marketing efforts and have them comment on what they think the message is that you are trying to convey. Ask them to comment on your office setup and how they feel about what they see as well as their overall experience. Money spent on a simple effort such as this will often yield very valuable feedback. While many people approach this concept by using their public relations consultant or media person, be careful to avoid this trap. While they may be highly skilled in the areas of branding, marketing, and advertising, in reality they are not your customers. You need a solid cross section of clients (both new and established) to truly identify how people see you. And show them your competitor's websites and ask them to compare them with you. And finally, reward them for their input and remind them that their constructive criticism is essential and will be used to better the overall patient experience.

2. Review your website traffic rankings by using a service such as ALEXA (www.alexa.com) . Unless you are MSN, Yahoo, or Google, your ranking is going to be much higher than 100,000. That's fine. But what you want to look at are the trends. Is your traffic ranking rising? Are there more people seeing your website now then there were over the prior 3 months. And do you have enough essential links? If you aren't seeing increased traffic, have your site evaluated by an SEO specialist. Simply having a website is not enough…you need a good website! Feel free to connect with us and we will help get you pointed in the right direction. Because you purchased this book, you will find a special offer at the end of this chapter that may help you in your initial efforts. And if you aren't interested in embarking on a full SEO project at this point, we can at least advise you on the basics of running a pay per click campaign that will help drive short term traffic to your website. And when you are ready, we would be happy to help construct an SEO campaign that will ultimately ensure an optimized organic effort with the major search engines.

3. Meet with your staff as soon as possible and meet on a regular basis. Meetings don't need to be lengthy and, in fact, should be brief and to the point. During these sessions, discuss with your staff how they currently interact with people in the client opportunity zone. What do they do when someone calls on the phone looking for information? What actions do they take when a customer asks them about a product or service complimentary to the one they are already buying? Your primary objective is to make sure that you don't lose client opportunities when they are in your office, on the phone, or when corresponding by email. And never assume that all members of your staff are equally good at this. Another critical early action is to have someone secret shop your office. Have a friend call and pose as a potential client. Feedback from this type of encounter is essential because no matter how much you spend on

branding, marketing, and advertising, you have 15 seconds or less to secure a client. If the interaction is anything less than positive, you just lost all value of your outreach efforts.

4. The first three actions are critical because they are all customer facing steps. And considering that the average customer is worth more than $2,000, you cannot afford to lose a single opportunity. After you have completed these steps, start following the processes we outlined in the book. Look at your capacity, analyze your profit per service-type, review staff member skill set inventory, appraise market pricing and your position in the market, optimize your website strategy, and if possible upgrade your brand. Although all of these steps can be done by you and your staff, we are always ready to assist in your efforts.

Special Book Owner's Promotion: Contract with us for consulting work to achieve a highly profitable continuously growing practice and we will give you an hour of consulting for every hour you purchase (up to 50 hours). That gets you a 40 hour consulting assignment in which we will completely review your brand, website, client opportunity zone strategy and execution, as well as help you setup processes that will keep you on top once we get you there: all for the price of a 20 hour engagement. Contact us at www.beautyandthebusinessbook.com for instructions on how to claim this valuable incentive.

Although we never recommend that you become a discounted service provider, we are prepared to prove ourselves by presenting this tremendous offer to you, the reader. We wish you the very best as you enter the exciting world of Aesthetic Medicine and are happy to answer any questions you may have along the way.

Warmest regards,

Greg & Steve

Contact Information:

Gregory A. Buford, MD FACS
BEAUTY by BUFORD
Kismet Communications, LLC
125 Inverness Drive East
Suite 200
Englewood, CO 80112
303.708.8234
greg@beautyandthebusinessbook.com

Steven E. House
Kismet Communications, LLC
125 Inverness Drive East
Suite 200
Englewood, CO 80112
303.708.8234
steve@beautyandthebusinessbook.com

ABOUT THE AUTHORS

Dr. Gregory A. Buford is a Board Certified Plastic Surgeon currently practicing in Denver, CO who was born and raised in Lake Oswego, OR. As a graduate of the Baker/Stuzin/Baker Cosmetic Surgery Fellowship in Miami, he is one of the few cosmetic plastic surgeons in the Rocky Mountain Region to have completed formal post-graduate training. Dr. Buford holds higher degrees from the Georgetown University School of Medicine and the University of California, San Diego where he received his major in Literature with an emphasis in writing. His practice is limited exclusively to Aesthetic Medicine with an emphasis on Breast Enhancement, Body Contouring, and Minimally Invasive Facial Rejuvenation. Because of this extensive background, he currently participates on a number of Advisory Councils for organizations such as Mentor Corporation and Allergan, Inc.

A nationally recognized judge for the Miss America Foundation and media and industry darling, Dr. Buford has been a featured expert on numerous television talk shows, plastic surgery websites, books, magazines, and newspapers. He has published several medical white papers on plastic surgery, and is a premier expert trainer in the industry responsible for leading CME courses and training seminars. He boasts a long list of accolades and accreditations, including features in New Beauty, Vogue, American Spa, ABCNews.com, RealSelf.com, Plastic Surgery Advisor, FOX television affiliates, healthology.com and emedicine.com as a respected industry resource for professional advice and training on plastic surgery and a number of the facial injectables. He is a nationally recognized speaker and consultant to Lumenis in addition to an acting co-director for the only Colorado-based National Training Center for Encore Fractional CO2 laser resurfacing.

As an advisor to the financial industry, he is a highly-respected top tier consultant to Gerson Lehrman Group on issues related to current and predicted future trends within the field of aesthetic medicine. In 2006, the Consumers' Research Council of America named him one of "America's Top Surgeons." He is an active participant in a number of non-profits and currently sits on the CultureHaus Board of Directors and is an alumni member of the Denver Active 20/30 Children's Foundation. He was recently named a finalist for "Champions of Healthcare" by the Denver Business Journal for his numerous charitable contributions. Time away from his practice is spent writing, cooking, practicing photography, collecting art & antiques, and enjoying Colorado's abundant outdoor pastimes.

Steven E. House was born and raised in Fowlerville Michigan. In 1981, he graduated from Ohio Institute of Technology with a degree in Electronic Engineering Technology and later obtained the degree of Bachelor of Science in Business from the University of Phoenix. Over a 28 year career, he has worked in software, software development and hardware technologies within the computer industry and has spent 26 of these years with a specific focus on the healthcare industry. This experience has been localized to both the acute care setting as well as the physician office environment and has included executive sales and marketing management. Steve has also owned and operated a medical billing business which allowed him to gain an acute knowledge of the medical office environment in multiple specialties. He is the President of Big House, Inc which owns and operates over 100 websites and provides search engine optimization services for a variety of industries. Steve is an award winning Toastmaster and highly compensated public speaker who has presented around the world to healthcare related audiences as well as to those seeking personal motivation.

BUY A SHARE OF THE FUTURE IN YOUR COMMUNITY

These certificates make great holiday, graduation and birthday gifts that can be personalized with the recipient's name. The cost of one S.H.A.R.E. or one square foot is $54.17. The personalized certificate is suitable for framing and will state the number of shares purchased and the amount of each share, as well as the recipient's name. The home that you participate in "building" will last for many years and will continue to grow in value.

Here is a sample SHARE certificate:

THIS CERTIFIES THAT

YOUR NAME HERE

HAS INVESTED IN A HOME FOR A DESERVING FAMILY

1985-2005

TWENTY YEARS OF BUILDING FUTURES IN OUR
COMMUNITY ONE HOME AT A TIME

1200 SQUARE FOOT HOUSE @ $65,000 = $54.17 PER SQUARE FOOT
This certificate represents a tax deductible donation. It has no cash value.

YES, I WOULD LIKE TO HELP!

I support the work that Habitat for Humanity does and I want to be part of the excitement! As a donor, I will receive periodic updates on your construction activities but, more importantly, I know my gift will help a family in our community realize the dream of homeownership. **I would like to SHARE in your efforts against substandard housing in my community!** *(Please print below)*

PLEASE SEND ME _____ SHARES at $54.17 EACH = $ $_____

In Honor Of: _____

Occasion: (Circle One)   HOLIDAY   BIRTHDAY   ANNIVERSARY

          OTHER: _____

Address of Recipient: _____

Gift From: _____ *Donor Address:* _____

Donor Email: _____

I AM ENCLOSING A CHECK FOR $ $_____ PAYABLE TO HABITAT FOR HUMANITY OR PLEASE CHARGE MY VISA OR MASTERCARD *(CIRCLE ONE)*

Card Number _____ Expiration Date: _____

Name as it appears on Credit Card _____ Charge Amount $ _____

Signature _____

Billing Address _____

Telephone # Day _____ Eve _____

PLEASE NOTE: Your contribution is tax-deductible to the fullest extent allowed by law.
Habitat for Humanity • P.O. Box 1443 • Newport News, VA 23601 • 757-596-5553
www.HelpHabitatforHumanity.org